THE FROG
IN YOUR
THROAT

THE FROG
IN YOUR
THROAT

SHERAL DEVAUGHN

"The Frog In Your Throat"
(An Unconventional Primer For L.E.A.P.ing Life's Hurdles)

Copyright © 2022 by Sheral DeVaughn

All rights reserved.

Published by
C3 Specialties
Kansas City, Missouri
www.SpeakingWithSher.com

Quantity discounts of this book are available. Personalized autographed copies are also available. Contact the publisher for more information and a quote.

Paperback ISBN: 979-8-218-06069-5
Library of Congress Control Number: 2022915689

Book Design by YellowStudios
First Edition

Printed in the United States of America

This book is dedicated to those who have felt like their voice didn't matter. The ones who felt unheard and invisible. The ones with a "frog in their throat" unsure of the hurdles. I am listening. I hear you.

To Christie for helping me get my "groove" back.

To my "ride or die" crew. "We're hell when we're well and we're hardly ever sick." I LOVE YOU MAN!!! You remind me daily that giving up is NEVER an option. Thank you for accepting me just the way I am.

To Julie for pushing me past my self-induced limitations.

To Lea, Princeton, Kevin, Tony & Lisa. You are the reasons I REMEMBER WHO I AM.

To Lauren for helping me pick up the pieces and put them back together.

To Gary for making me feel "safe" within my inner-child space again.

To my husband Chris. Thank you for having the unconditional belief, love, and patience to help me see this through.

To my daughters Katy and Devon who helped me define my purpose. This book is for you. NEVER forget how important your voice is and always will be.

To my mother, who didn't get to see this day. I should have written this book for you long ago. I miss you.

To my brother, Scott. I hope this gives you some answers and insight on how I made it through. You can make it too.

FOREWORD

How can a fish, frog, and stork teach you about solving life's problems? You will have to read *The Frog in your Throat* by Sheral DeVaughn to find out. I am so excited to share this book with the world. As a media personality and fellow book author, I am often asked to write forewords for many new authors. Most of the time, I politely decline. But not this time! The best way to describe this is that it's the Un-Fairytale for Adults. Sheral has a fabulous sense of humor and can harness that while still sharing some pretty dark times.

This book is an excellent read for those of us who are struggling with life. Sheral writes with wit and humor about the reality of life and how we need to take control of our destiny through self-care and self-discovery.

The Frog in Your Throat is one of the best books I have read this year. It was so relatable in all aspects of life, whether you are a parent, an employee, or anything else. The author has such a fantastic way of teaching and educating people in a fun and entertaining way. I would recommend this book to anyone who wants to enjoy more of life with a bit less struggle.

"Finding your voice may be what helps us all live happily ever after, even if it's just with ourselves."

Lea Woodford
www.SmartFem.com

CONTENTS

INTRODUCTION

Have you ever felt like no one could hear you? Like you had an "invisible voice?"

It's the type of voice where when you speak, no one acknowledges it. You can say something that everyone ignores, but when someone else says the same thing, it's met with approval.

Or maybe you're afraid to speak up. Worried about being judged or ridiculed. Nervous that the words won't come out right, so you don't say anything at all. You have "a frog in your throat."

But that frog never goes away. It stays lodged, waiting to come out.

How many times have you caught yourself wishing things had gone differently in your life? You think about goals and dreams you once had and think to yourself, "If only…"

You reminisce, daydream, and sigh longingly for the days when you "might've done something differently." You complain, you get sad or frustrated, and then resolve yourself to accepting an unsatisfying and unremarkable way of living.

There are a million reasons why you can't get over the hurdle that has been so rudely put in your path. Everything ranging from "I'm too old" and "I don't have enough time" to "I was born into this situation" and "Someone else is standing in my way."

Yet there are those that somehow overcome the hurdles. They cross the finish line to their own personal and professional success. Are they just lucky? Is their situation different than anyone else's set of circumstances? Maybe they just were born as extraordinary individuals.

The truth is, we all can turn our obstacles into opportunities. A slight shift in your mindset is all it takes to change your direction and bring you closer to your goals. It doesn't matter your age, your finances, or any other factor. It only depends on you.

What if I could show you how "the frog in your throat" is a GOOD thing? It's what you need to get your voice heard. In fact, it's exactly the thing you need to get past the hurdles to create the life you were meant to live.

It took me decades of hurdles, destructive behaviors, and hard lessons to finally get to the life I've been looking for. A life I didn't think I'd find. A life I didn't think I was worthy of living.

I'd like to share with you what I've learned along the way while getting over my own hurdles so that you can select and adapt what works for you to get over your own hurdles.

CHAPTER 1

THE NATURE OF LIFE'S BEASTS

The best way to explain how this works (at least for me) is to turn what seems to be an overwhelming and complicated idea into something simpler and approachable.

For me, this involves acronyms and animals. An unlikely combination, but one that even kids can understand.

Let's start with those hurdles life throws at you. Each of those seemingly insurmountable challenges is what I refer to as a **S.T.O.R.K.** (Situational Taker of Rational Knowledge).

The **S.T.O.R.K.**, much like the obstacles you face in life, doesn't care how you feel or if what is happening is fair. It hovers over you, casting shadows of doubt on your abilities. It takes away your ability to think through a situation and realize there are always solutions. The **S.T.O.R.K.** will find you and swallow you whole if you allow it to do so.

The people most affected and swallowed alive are the **F.I.S.H.** (Folks in Search of Help).

They're like most people; swimming along in their own waters, minding the business of their day-to-day lives. And then out of nowhere…

…they find themselves staring into the jaws of the **S.T.O.R.K.**

When these challenges and obstacles hit, **F.I.S.H.** don't fight, they fall prey to the situation. They look for someone or something to come along and save them. **F.I.S.H.** will ignore the problem, avoid it, lament the situation, and ultimately accept that there is nothing they can do to change their unfortunate outcome.

Not everyone remains a victim of their circumstances, however. There are those who get over the initial shock of being hit with one of life's hurdles and decide they aren't going to let it take control.

These individuals are what I call a **F.R.O.G.** (Folks Refusing Other's Garbage). Because let's face it, that's what these setbacks are- GARBAGE- that belong somewhere else and not with you.

The **F.R.O.G.** understands that a hurdle isn't a permanent stopping force. You can go over it, around it, under it. You can knock it down, fall on it, and crawl across it. No matter how you choose to make your way forward, there is ALWAYS a way past it and a way to prevent the **S.T.O.R.K.** from swallowing you alive. When things get hard the **F.R.O.G.** digs in and fights to find a solution that may not be apparent at first glance. A **F.R.O.G.** doesn't wait for someone else to save him.

The **F.R.O.G.** refuses to give up.

How does one go from being a **F.I.S.H.** to a **F.R.O.G.**?

There are two ways:

1. **C.R.O.A.K.** (Challenge Really Obnoxious A-holes and Kill-Joys)
2. **L.E.A.P.** (Look/Learn, Educate/Evolve, Act, Practice/Participate)

How do I know this? Any of this?

I have lived it and experienced how it directly impacted my life, my dreams, and my happiness/success.

Now I want to show you how you can apply it and do the same in your life.

Let's get hopping, shall we?

CHAPTER 2

THE INVISIBLE VOICE

"Once upon a time."

Isn't that how all stories are supposed to begin? At least the fairy tales do, where the princess faces a villain or a tragedy and loses all the things promised to her, but in the end, a handsome knight or prince shows up to save the day, and they all live happily ever after. They even get talking animals.

But my life wasn't a fairy tale, and I certainly wasn't born a princess.

I grew up in rural Minnesota during the '70s and '80s. Most people in the area never ventured far or had aspirations of greatness. You married someone locally, had a few kids, and kept everything status quo. In my family, at least on my dad's side, the status quo for the women and girls was living as the support staff for our "men." We didn't have a whole lot of value other than cooking, cleaning, and making babies. If we worked, we worked for the benefit of the men. Our opinions weren't wanted. Heck, we didn't even get to pick who we dated (I spent an awful lot of time sneaking out windows after coming home early from my "pre-selected date").

We were supposed to be seen (on occasion) and not heard. When we didn't behave the way we were expected to, we were met by roars of drunken disapproval at best, violent fits of anger and abuse on the worst of days. Princes and chivalrous knights they were not. Happily ever after was replaced by surviving and making the best of what you had. No one was coming to rescue anyone. More often than not, everyone turned a blind eye and pretended nothing had happened. It was a community full of people who had learned to never speak up and let their voice be heard unless you were the town bully. A community of **F.I.S.H.** It just so happened my family was the town royalty of bullies.

As irony would have it, I didn't get the memo regarding what was expected of the girls in the family. I was born with a bit of a mouth, a lot of attitude, and a desire to entertain. Little sassy Sheral. It was cute up until about the age of 7 or 8. My family looked at me as sort of the favorite pet. I was smart, charming, and performed on command. And when I was finished entertaining their friends and visiting family members, I'd be rewarded with ice cream and silver dollars before being sent off to disappear out of sight once again. It was a good gig for a while. But even in childhood, the day comes when you realize you deserve more. That day came when I decided to own my name and my independence, declaring my name was not Sheri, but Sheral, and I would no longer answer to anything else. Without realizing it, that was my first attempt at being a **F.R.O.G.** I chose to **C.R.O.A.K.** at my grandfather and the rest of my family.

It didn't go quite as I had planned.

My days of ice cream and silver dollars were over. Little did I know that would be the start of the end of the relationship with my dad's side of the family. I was sent to my room and ostracized from then on.

What I didn't know then was that it wasn't enough to **C.R.O.A.K.** Using the voice inside of you to stand up for yourself and declare your intentions is only the first part of the process. You must be willing to not only use that invisible voice inside of you to tell others what is acceptable and what is not, but you need to be willing to act accordingly to back up your declaration and see it through.

There were two choices for me: Silence my voice and accept that I would never be allowed to be anything more than "just another girl" in the family. My days of being the favorite "pet" were over, so I was just another female number.

Or I could come up with a plan to get me out of my situation and escape a life that was intolerable.

I chose the latter and spent more time in my tiny bedroom than I spent just about anywhere else. I wasn't about to silence my voice, but I also wasn't going to chance being beaten for not following "the rules."

Your way over the hurdles and past the **S.T.O.R.K.** won't always happen quickly nor easily. Sometimes you won't even realize what the answer is even when it's right there in front of you. That was the case for me.

Hours added up to days and years locking myself away in my bedroom. I replaced family interaction with a bunch of stuffed animals, and an old radio. The friendly voices that spoke to me from that radio during those days were exciting, full of fun, and full of possibilities. I hung on every word from my "new friends", the legendary Wolfman Jack (yes, I am dating myself) and my "Weekly" buddy Casey Kasem. If you don't know who I'm talking about, The Wolfman was in movies like "American Graffiti" and Rob Zombie's movie "31." Casey Kasem was the original voice of "The Weekly Top 40" before Ryan Seacrest was a glimmer in his Mama's eye. Another fun fact: Casey was the original voice of Shaggy in the Scooby-Doo cartoons. I delighted in the thought of Shaggy counting down my favorite songs each week.

Those radio DJs spoke in a way that made me believe they were speaking DIRECTLY to me. As though they could hear my thoughts. They understood how to truly connect with another human being. It's something I refer to as *"The Power of a 5 Minute Conversation."* - You never know what sort of impact your words can have on a person that changes their life…even if it's a total stranger, or in this case, someone they would never meet.

I had dreams of becoming as successful as they were. I would stand in front of my mirror with a hairbrush and play my vinyl 45 records on a little "Close and Play" record player. I practiced my delivery in that mirror, but I also had conversations with myself regarding what I was going to do, how to do it, and how I would "show everyone" when I made it.

Those *5-minute Conversations* with yourself are every bit as powerful as the ones you have with others. They are the first step in growing your confidence, communicating your worth, and being able to have your voice heard. You need to be able to hear your own voice, to recognize how important and powerful it truly is before anyone else will listen.

CHAPTER 3

LEARNING TO L.E.A.P.

I can hear it now. "Sher (that's what my friends call me, and I'd like to think we'll be friends by the end of this book), that's a fun story about a kid wanting to pursue her dreams, but how does that help me get over life's hurdles?"

That's where part two comes in; the **L.E.A.P.** portion of the plan.

L.E.A.P.ing over a hurdle doesn't have to be a complicated thing, nor is it only for a special group of overachievers.

It's simple enough for a 10-year-old to figure out.

"But Sher, how tough can the hurdles of a 10-year-old be?"

Pretty tough for a kid born with issues and born into circumstances beyond her control. I know, that sounds like an excuse for why some hurdles are just too high to **L.E.A.P.** over.

But sometimes those hurdles provide the motivation and opportunity for your growth and success.

Let's go back to my situation.

I was stuck in a family and a town that wasn't going to give me a happy life. That was apparent even as a little kid.

So, I needed to figure out a way to either:

    a) make my family, friends, and the good people of my hometown see that I was so much more than "just a girl"

    b) find a way out of the town.

Most girls looked for someone to come along and sweep them off their feet so they could live happily ever after.

That wasn't in the cards for me.

First of all, boys were "icky" (come on, I was 10!) and secondly, any boy had to meet with the approval of my dad. That wasn't going to improve my circumstances any.

Plus, I had already decided I was going to grow up to be the female version of Wolfman Jack. There was one glaring problem I was going to have to overcome before that could happen.

I had a speech impediment.

I couldn't say words with 'ng' in them correctly.

"Hanger", "singing", and "bang" sounded like "hay-nur", "sinnin'", and "bane".

My word pronunciation had become the "bane" of my existence.

It's a big ask to become a legendary DJ when you can't pronounce your words.

Kids made fun of me. I didn't have many friends. I didn't want to talk. I was embarrassed.

The school wouldn't set me up with their speech therapist because I was one of the "gifted" students. Apparently "smart" kids didn't need to speak well according to the administration.

Most people would come to terms with the fact that life had decided that their position going forward would be that of a **F.I.S.H.**

But I wasn't a **F.I.S.H.** I was more of a tadpole…still developing those **L.E.A.P**.ing legs. I knew there had to be a solution. I just hadn't found it yet.

It could be done. Just because you're born with or develop an issue doesn't mean you have to be stuck with it.

Both Marilyn Monroe and James Earl Jones had stutters.

Yes, Darth Vader stutters while trying to take over the Galaxy. Even to this day.

If they could find a way surely I could too.

Sometimes the way presents itself with the assistance of another **F.R.O.G.** This isn't someone who is rushing in solely to save someone out of the goodness of their heart. Their intentions MIGHT be good, but they're most likely one of those **F**olks **R**efusing **O**ther's **G**arbage.

And my impediment was garbage.

My encounter with another **F.R.O.G.** came packaged as Sally Halbmaier, another gifted student and classmate of mine who became my spelling partner.

Sally wasn't exactly a fan of mine in the 5th grade (although we would become good friends over the years). My impediment drove her bonkers.

She was a skilled problem-solver, however, and my first real-life introduction to **L.E.A.P**.

She **LOOKED** at the problem: she hated listening to me mispronounce my words.

She **EDUCATED** me on how to correct it: I was to overpronounce a variety of 'ng' words each night for 30 minutes, consistently increasing the speed until it came out correctly ("Hane-gur", "banguh", "Singuh-inguh"). This was brilliant and a technique I use to this day.

ACTION was taken: each day we had spelling she would quiz me to see how I was progressing. If I mispronounced a word, she'd smack me with our spelling book.

PRACTICE was encouraged: I made darn sure I was putting in at LEAST 30 minutes each night on pronunciations. Let's face it, Sally was athletic, and that spelling book didn't feel good. It took me about 2 weeks to meet with her approval. Thank goodness spelling wasn't every day!

While I'm not an advocate of grade school corporal punishment to effectively get you over life's hurdles, it does highlight that even a child can come up with solutions to seemingly impossible challenges.

If 10-year-old Sally Halbmaier can be a **F.R.O.G.** and think outside the box to **L.E.A.P.** over the problem, anyone can find a way. She didn't give up, and neither should you.

By the way, if Sally is reading this, or if anyone happens to know how to reach her, please know that I am forever grateful to you for the gift you gave me back in Mrs. Hafslund's classroom. Genuinely.

CHAPTER 4

WHEN YOU DON'T HAVE A LEG TO STAND ON

You're likely thinking to yourself, "Maybe that **F.RO.G./ L.E.A.P.** thing works for kids, but I'm not a grade school kid. I have real issues that came out of nowhere."

And you likely do. Often, the **S.T.O.R.K.**'s gifts are surprises that can knock us off our feet. Quite literally.

What happens if you're suddenly faced with an injury or a disability? What if it happens just as you're in, or coming into your prime?

You find yourself unable to do the things you had planned. Sometimes it's a minor thing, but how do you **L.E.A.P.** over a hurdle if you can literally no longer **L.E.A.P.** at all? Do you give up?

Of course not. After all, if you're this far along, you're not a **F.I.S.H.**, you're a **F.R.O.G.**

Look at former NFL Quarterback Alex Smith. In 2018, the 16-year, Pro Bowl QB suffered a devasting leg break during a game. The same injury that ended Joe Theismann's career back in 1985.

As if that wasn't enough, Smith would end up with a life-threatening, flesh-eating bacterial infection. After 17 surgeries in 9 months, doctors told him he would never play again and would likely lose his leg.

In 2020 he would return to the field, throw a career high game, and be named the NFL Comeback Player of the Year. He has since gone on to be a sports analyst for ESPN.

Smith is an extreme example of determination and a never give up attitude.

You don't have to be a high-performance athlete to suffer a life-changing injury and make a comeback though.

In October of 1984 I was in high school. No longer burdened with that speech impediment (Thanks Sally!), I was enjoying a large circle of friends. I was a starter on the volleyball and softball teams. I was getting leads in the theater plays and musicals. I had an older boyfriend. Why yes, he WAS chosen by my dad, but hanging with the older crowd was still seen as a status thing- at least in my eyes. I was living a pretty good life for a teenage kid. Like most, I wasn't worried so much about my career goals and dreams as I was wondering what movie I was going to see that weekend.

One night after theater rehearsal, I was walking out of the school to wait for my ride. There was a thin layer of black ice just outside the door on the sidewalk. I remember spinning and falling. I remember what sounded like the muffled sound of a stick cracking. I remember seeing bone sticking through my sock. I don't remember much of that night after that.

I ended up with a compound fracture of the right ankle. It had broken in 4 places and come through the skin. Unfortunately, it had also torn through and shredded the ligaments. We wouldn't know how badly it was damaged until the cast came off in January. Surgery was scheduled for February. Valentine's Day of 1985. They would split the tendon in the bottom of my foot and staple half of it to the bone where the ligaments had been. It would be ugly for a while, but it would heal, and I could go back to normal.

Normal never came.

There wasn't much to love after the procedure on this "Day of Romance." I woke up in post-op, groggy, wondering how much pain I would feel and how heavy the cast would be. I lifted the right leg with ease. No pain, light weight, no issues. When I lifted the left leg to compare, that's when the **S.T.O.R.K.** arrived. An entire surgical team of 7 didn't realize they had operated on the wrong leg until they heard me shrieking in the recovery room.

That wasn't the end of the mistakes that day. They would proceed to give me a double dose of anesthesia and put me under again to quickly operate on the correct leg. They would do a shoddy job all the way around.

I spent the better part of a month in the hospital being monitored for pneumonia thanks to all the anesthesia. I would learn how to get myself in and out of a bed, use a bathroom, get dressed, and properly use a wheelchair since both legs would remain in casts and be non-weight bearing.

I was only 16, and I would spend the next 6 years in and out of wheelchairs and casts. I would undergo another 4 surgeries: 2 to remove the staples my body was rejecting, and 2 to sever the nerves the staples in both legs had gone through. I would no longer have feeling in my feet. I would likely lose the ability to walk well, or at all, by the time I was 50 due to degeneration from the damage. I would always have to battle my own sort of PTSD for even the smallest medical procedure.

No more high school sports. No more dances. No more roller skating or ski trips with friends.

I would be limited with theater, with being the high school mascot, heck, I would be unable to get to many of my classes for months because the school wasn't handicapped accessible and I couldn't navigate steps, bathrooms, nor even the desks.

My grades would plummet, my friendships would suffer, my mental health would suffer.

My mother was a saint through all of this. She would run herself ragged trying to work with me, keep my spirits up, serving as the go-between and tutor for my schoolwork, and trying to get me to any extracurricular activity she could think of to make me feel included. But my mom was also a **F.I.S.H.** and believed that someone, somewhere, was going to fix her child and help her with the burden of helping me to function. She needed the help with a grade school son and my dad who suffered from a paralyzing back injury. She just kept swimming and waiting. I knew no one was coming to help, so I had to be the one to **L.E.A.P.** into action.

I worked hard over the next year to get back on my feet (literally). I relearned how to walk based on where my knees locked. I built up my muscle strength. Despite not feeling my feet, I could run, skate, dance, and move normally again in between the surgeries and physical therapy. In fact, I would schedule surgeries for off-season, so I'd be able to participate fully in the activities I loved and work most of the summer as a lifeguard. Everything was planned to the minute. I was ready to go back to normal. I needed it to go back to normal.

But coaches wouldn't let me play on the sports teams, directors were afraid to let me have acting parts that required much physicality. The school wouldn't allow me to ever do the things fully I had done before out of fear of added injuries that might lead to lawsuits. They effectively took everything away from me again.

This could have easily been a time when I could have turned into a **F.I.S.H.** No one would have blamed me. I could have just blended into the background and become a spectator in life. It was what I saw so many others do. It was what my mom was doing. I would have had a lot of company swimming with me.

But there is always a way to **L.E.A.P.**, even if it's not the path you originally chose, in which to move forward.

STEP 1 was to **LOOK/LEARN**: If I couldn't do things physically, what other opportunities were available for me?

I could still use my voice. I could still do theater in most capacities, and I could join the speech/debate team.

STEP 2 was to **EDUCATE/EVOLVE**: How could I learn to do this well where it made a difference? What made the best speakers and actors so much better than the others? I would check out books, watch television shows, study news anchors, and pour over movies (we didn't have a lot of access to computers or anything like Google when I was in high school) to see if I could pick up any patterns.

I discovered that they all:

    a) Made themselves approachable so others were comfortable around them.

    b) Learned what was important and interesting to their target audience for relatability.

c) Used tone, facial expressions, and gestures to convey whatever emotion or attribute they wanted to communicate to whomever they were speaking to.

d) Spoke to others in a way that was confident and conveyed a sense of authority without being overbearing.

They had mastered the ability to CONNECT through their communication. It was pure, unadulterated POWER…and I wanted to have it. It was almost an obsession and addiction once it clicked in my head because it was the only way I could see to stop being helpless and powerless.

STEP 3 was to **ASSESS/ACT**: I spent most of my time surrounding myself with people I thought were the best examples of that style of speaking. Teachers, coaches, businesspeople. I watched and listened to the styles of the other students who were competing in speech and in theater, making notes of what was effective and what wasn't. I looked at what I was doing and incorporated the pieces that worked for me into my personality and delivery style. I even decided to get rid of my Minnesota accent since none of the news anchors nor celebrities seemed to sound like where they were from.

STEP 4 was to **PRACTICE/PARTICIPATE**: I auditioned for every theater performance available and signed up for every speech tournament offered. I spent hours every day after school working with my coaches (until they finally got sick of me or sent me home) and at least an hour every day at home practicing in front of that same mirror I used to speak into pretending to be a DJ. This wasn't pretend anymore though. This was my future.

By the time I was a senior in high school I wasn't just good at it, I was exceptional. I was one of the best in the state for both theater and speech competitions. I had a room full of trophies and medallions. I had even parlayed it into winning the ever-prestigious title of Miss Belle Plaine (which meant I was a glorified sloppy joe queen for our annual BBQ Days event in our little town). I had scholarships for college.

I thought I had "shown them all."

Ah, to be young, dumb and "bulletproof."

What it really did was provide me with another tool to defeat the **S.T.O.R.K.**s.

When you can't **L.E.A.P.** a hurdle in a conventional way, find an unconventional method to keep you moving forward towards your goals and successes. It might not happen instantaneously, and it won't always come easily. But it will come if you decide there is no other alternative.

Be the **F.R.O.G.** and never give up.

CHAPTER 5

THEY DON'T TEACH YOU THESE THINGS IN COLLEGE

"Yo, Sheral, that's all great for kids and young adults. I can even see where it could help someone with an injury. But I'm an adult with a job, a family, and a boss. I'm just a cog in the machine working for "the man." If you do a good job, work hard, and don't stir up any trouble, things should be alright. Plus, you can't really fight against your boss if you want to stay employed. I don't see how any of this could apply to me."

I hear you.

But this is where you NEED to be the **F.R.O.G.** more than ever. It's the most important time to know how to **C.R.O.A.K.** and **L.E.A.P.** Because this, my friend, is where the **S.T.O.R.K.** begins to look like Godzilla or one of those big mob bosses in your video games. And it comes with the frequency of stomach upset after eating too many fast-food tacos.

Life doesn't care if you're playing nice. It doesn't care if you're following whatever rules you think will keep you out of harm's way. It will hit you indiscriminately, and it will hit you as hard as Sally Halbmaier could swing a spelling book. Probably harder.

After finishing my 4 years of college and completing a media internship, I packed up everything and moved to Shreveport, Louisiana to be with my soon-to-be-husband Chris. I was still going to be a radio star. At 23 you still have dreams, and you don't have the experiences that show you you're going to have mountainous hurdles ahead. I was young and bullet proof, overconfident, and capable in my own mind. Like so many today who make the same claim, I knew what my worth was.

But life doesn't care what you THINK you're worth. And quite frankly it laughs at your self-appraised value.

I managed to get hired on by a Public Radio Station locally to get a feel for the market. It was a good first gig. It gave me a chance to polish up my skills with the equipment and gave me a bit of experience. Doing a 2-hour weekly show back at the college station I had attended wasn't exactly the stuff of dream resumés, so I gladly took the full-time position and waited for an opening at a commercial station to open. I knew that public radio wasn't going to give me the chance to let my DJ personality shine.

My opportunity came just under a year later. It was a part-time position doing overnights on the weekends. It wasn't great, but it was a chance to get my foot in the door and prove I had what it took to move into bigger and better on-air slots. The only thing standing in the way of me getting the position? It was at a Country station. Not just Country, but Country AND Western. I was a Duran-Duran and Devo kind of a gal. I couldn't tell you the difference between Tanya

Tucker and Friar Tuck when it came to the music. It was time to put **L.E.A.P.** into action and get myself familiarized enough with Country music so I could ace my interview.

I refer to that 48 hours as "*My Weekend with David Allen Coe*" or "*How to Deal with the Loss of Your Dog, Truck, and Mama at the Train Station.*" Our friend Dennis had an extensive CD collection of classic and current country artists. Outside of 7 hours of sleep each night, I did nothing for two days but listen to, and get quizzed on, the country artists and their songs. It worked. I got hired.

For the next 6 months, I would get calls from listeners like "Dusty." This guy would call me every Saturday morning at 2 am to tell me he loved listening to the sound of my voice as he was lying in bed... wearing his Underoos. As disturbing as it was to have a grown man tell me he was listening while wearing cartoon underwear, I felt like it was a fair trade off for the education and experience I was getting. I was **L.E.A.P**.ing into action. I was **LEARNING** about the listeners, what they liked to do, what was important to them, and how best to relate to them. I would come in during the week to **EDUCATE** myself on commercial production and audio editing techniques. I **ASSESSED** that I had a talent for it. Management noticed it too. So, I **PRACTICED** and **PARTICIPATED** more by accepting more opportunities. I would fill in frequently during the week for the full-time staff. I was getting more and more commercial assignments. In just 6 months I would be ready to make my power move. The current morning show female and acting program director had left. While they brought in a new PD, they still needed to find a female co-host for the #1 show in the market. Auditions opened and I applied. I made the call-backs and was given a trial-run with the male host of the show. It went beautifully and 2 days later they announced I got the job.

At 25 years of age, and with under 2 years of radio experience, I was now the co-host for the #1 morning show in the market. I was caught up in the excitement of the newspaper interviews and the professional photos. So caught up that I didn't notice the warning signs. This wasn't going to be my superstar moment.

If you recall, I mentioned that they had hired a new Program Director. I was familiar with his background as he had done morning radio back where I grew up. He was friendly enough and complimentary prior to my landing of the co-host position. He would often tell stories of his own experiences in radio. Typical radio ego. Nothing that was surprising. What I didn't pay attention to were some of the 'red flag' comments.

After hiring me for the position, he made it a point to tell me that I "scored a B+" in the audition, but it was still better than the others and, besides that, I would make my morning co-host "look good." That should have tipped me off, but at 25 and having no experience in the industry, you don't understand some of the politics at play. At that time, women in radio were seen more as sidekicks to their male counterparts in morning radio. The woman I was replacing was an exception to that rule, and I certainly hadn't realized it might be any different. I should have.

It took approximately 3 months before I saw what was happening. I wasn't hired to be an equal partner on the show. I was hired to be "the sweet young sidekick who looked good" in photos next to "the star of the show."

At month 4 I was incredibly frustrated. I began to **C.R.O.A.K.** because I was surrounded by **OBNOX-IOUS A-HOLES AND KILL-JOYS**. The radio industry was (and in some ways, still is) a very male-dominated industry. I had become the butt of jokes for what was a "good old boys' network." If they weren't mocking me, they were being dismissive and disapproving. It was prevalent. From the sales staff to the news guy. From the on-air talent to the Program Director, straight to the top with the General Manager. There wasn't a safe place to turn to voice my displeasure, downright anger, and hurt.

In fact, voicing my issues is when the volume was turned up to 11 on the problems I would face. Cartoons began appearing on my desk full of blatant sexual innuendo, harassment, and hostility. It was meant to be intimidating and belittling. My morning show partner would typically arrive before I did, and I would ask repeatedly if he had seen the materials or knew who was behind it. His answer was always one of denial, dismissal, and disinterest. For all I know, he might have been a participant. Nothing with any of them would have surprised me. Reporting it to human resources and management got me responses such as "the boys probably are just teasing you because they like you" and "you need to get some thicker skin." They would look into it. They never did.

It was demoralizing, but I wasn't about to quit. That's what they wanted me to do. I wasn't allowed to have input on the direction of the show. I wasn't being given live remotes nor endorsement opportunities. I wasn't even asked to sit in on show critiques. My "partner" was consulted. I was told I wasn't needed.

It got so bad that my partner wouldn't even turn on my microphone (he ran the board that controlled what was going out over the air). I'd be allowed to do the top of the hour ID, give the time and weather updates, but that was pretty much it. There were not-so-quiet rumblings that they were trying to finalize details to bring back the woman I had replaced. I knew it was only a matter of time before they got tired of waiting for me to leave on my own.

As miserable as it was, I needed the extra time to figure out a plan. I couldn't just quit because I was under a non-compete clause. That meant I couldn't go to work at any radio station within a 75-mile radius for a year once employment was terminated for any reason. It was part of my contract...a clause I would never forget moving forward and would fight against vehemently in subsequent contracts. I couldn't leave the market either. Chris was active-duty military stationed at Barksdale Air Force Base. Leaving my husband to pursue radio positions in other markets wasn't going to happen. There weren't any other acceptable options for me if I wanted to continue in the profession. So, I stayed, endured, and waited.

It wouldn't take long for life to make the decision for me. I got called into the General Manager's office to have a meeting with he and my program director. The day had finally come. I was being terminated. I knew it before I even got to the door of the office. My partner couldn't even make eye contact with me once our show was over (yes, they had me finish the show on a Friday before telling me I wasn't going to be keeping it. Standard in the business, honestly). The hallways got quiet, and eyes stared with sideways glances when I came close. It was hard not to notice the hushed whispers as I passed people. Everyone had already got the memo that I was gone. Everyone but me, officially.

They were cutting me loose and bringing back the old gal. The gal who had originally hired me. The gal who had already had a following in the market with my partner. The one who hadn't done so well in her new position and new market (or so I had been told). The one who had actively gone behind my back to remove me so she could jump back in. The one who had betrayed me. Who am I kidding? They all had betrayed me. Radio is filled with sharks. You either learn to swim with them or you get eaten. I had learned it the hard way.

I sat down across from the GM and waited for the door to close. When asked if I knew why I was there and how I felt I was doing in my position, I wanted to laugh. Instead, I just cut to the chase. "I have given my best despite not being allowed to do much. It hasn't been pleasant for a while, but I have given 100% regardless. I'm here because you're firing me from my position and bringing back the old co-host. It's been a great learning experience and I appreciate the opportunity. Will you be moving me into a different position?" Keep in mind, I was still trying to figure out a way to stay in the industry and keep building up. I had goals and this was the #1 station in town.

They could have simply just told me they didn't have a position for me and that our time together professionally was over. We would have parted ways and that would have been the end of it. But these two were the KINGS of **OB-NOXIOUS A-HOLES AND KILL-JOYS.** They couldn't miss an opportunity to humiliate and demoralize me one last time. They wanted to watch me walk out in tears. They wanted to see me completely broken.

They got the tears, but it wasn't because I was broken. I was pissed. I really wish I didn't cry when I get mad. But I do, and I was furious. I'm just happy they couldn't hear the dialogue that was taking place in my head. The General Manager explained to me in no uncertain terms that he thought I had no on-air talent. My Program Director agreed and wasn't sure why I had ever been put in the position in the first place. Um…hello. You both made the decision to put me there. You made the decision after I had been working as an on-air talent on your radio station for months beforehand, and AFTER I beat out 8 others in a live on-air audition with your morning show co-host.

That's when they made their mistake. The GM told me not only did I have no talent, but that I wasn't funny. I needed to go home, be a housewife, and buy a joke book so maybe I could learn how to tell a knock-knock joke properly. This was met with laughter and the approval of the Program Director…butt-kissing stooge that he was.

That's also when the **F.R.O.G.** in me saw the opportunity. I told them they were probably right, but it had always been my dream to be a radio personality. Since Chris was active duty and I couldn't move, would they be willing to drop the non-compete clause, in writing, so that I could go to work at some small farm station in Keithville or Sarepta and practice, perhaps on a part-time basis? I wasn't sure I'd ever get an opportunity at another station in town, but I knew I'd NEVER get it if I didn't get rid of that non-compete clause.

To my surprise, they gave it to me. They saw me as no threat whatsoever and decided it was the least they could do.

After all, even if I managed to find some backwoods station willing to hire me, it couldn't hurt them.

The meeting ended, and I went back to my former office to pack up my stuff. Someone was nice enough to have left an empty box for me on my desk to carry out my things. My old partner was nowhere to be found. I could guess who left me such a "thoughtful" gift. So, I loaded it not just with my personal items, but with the show prep I had put together for months…and all the other items for the morning show I had handled. Listener info, birthdays, etc. It was my work, and I wasn't about to give it up. They hadn't cared about it while I was there. Why would they care about it once I was gone? Besides, I knew I was going to need it for my next position even if I didn't know where or what that position would be. It was just a matter of time. I took my box, picked up my written non-compete waiver, and walked out for what I thought would be the last time.

What can you learn from this experience? Keep your emotions in check as best as you can, even when it appears the **S.T.O.R.K.** is on the verge of swallowing you whole. It's a task that's easier said than done, but if you do, you'll be able to see and seize the opportunity that will prevent you from being just another snack on life's plate. It might take time to utilize that one small piece or gift, but if you don't keep it together emotionally (even just a little bit), you might miss the chance to snatch it altogether.

Be the **F.R.O.G.** Never give up…even when you think you've lost it all. What you've been looking for is likely just around the corner. You might not even realize you were looking for it when you find it. In some cases, it might have been looking for you!

CHAPTER 6

THE FOCUSED F.R.O.G.

While it might have sounded like I was untouchable coming out of that situation, and ready to conquer the world, I was far from it. Just because we can choose to act like a **F.R.O.G.**, it doesn't mean it comes naturally or remains with us 24/7. People go through transformations much like a **F.R.O.G.** changes over time to leave the **F.I.S.H**./tadpole stage of its development. I was young with limited life experience. I had a taste of what I THOUGHT was my dream come true, and it didn't turn out the way I had planned. My first experience…my first major professional hurdle…left me with a lot of self-doubts. What if they had been right about me? What if I wasn't meant to do big things?

The chance to find out came about a month after I was unceremoniously fired from the #1 station in town. A format change was coming to one of the established radio stations. A new "young country" station. They were looking to hire for a midday position.

I figured I had nothing to lose. I had a morning show under my belt, I knew country music inside out, I was young and known in the market, and I could do commercial production.

I also wasn't tethered by a non-compete clause. Both the station owner and Program Director agreed I was a good fit.

Things were good. I was happy to be in a place without drama. At least I didn't think there was any drama. Everyone was happy, helpful, and talented. My goal was to soak up as much information and experience as I could, work hard, not rock the boat, and deliver the best show possible. I was grateful for the opportunity and thrilled to be appreciated in my capacity.

And deliver I did. The ratings came back strong in my time slot. My energy and skills were about to be rewarded once again. The station owner had decided he wanted to breathe life back into a morning show on his other station…a light rock station. He had decided to remove the female co-host from a long-established team and bring her on to do mornings on the new country stations. The idea was that there would be an established and well-known host on both stations by splitting the team apart. He thought it would strengthen both shows.

I would be taking her spot at the other station…AND keeping the midday spot I currently held. I was ecstatic! Apparently, I was the only one who was happy about the news.

The one thing that most people don't understand is that when things are going well for you, you are likely the **S.T.O.R.K.** for someone else. You may not be trying to be, and you may not even be aware of it, but it happens, nevertheless. It never occurred to me that I could be someone else's hurdle. Even if I had understood it, it likely wouldn't have made a difference in how things would play out, but it might have changed the way I looked at them and how I handled things as they happened.

I made people angry even though I wasn't making the decisions.

My Program Director wasn't happy that his established morning show was being broken apart and that he would be "coaching" an unseasoned commodity.

The current female co-host wasn't happy that she was being replaced and moved to what she considered a "lesser" position on the new station.

My soon-to-be new co-host wasn't thrilled about being paired with a new partner...and one that he had never met before.

Co-workers from both stations weren't impressed that I was taking opportunities they thought they should have a chance at. Not just one on-air time slot, but two.

The old station that fired me wasn't happy about me suddenly showing up weeks after parting ways with them in a competing morning show.

One of the things that can happen to you as you find yourself **L.E.A.P.**ing over numerous hurdles is that you start battling it instead of finding your way past it. You try to beat them into submission thinking you can make them go away and prevent them from ever returning. If you just do this one thing, or if you just explain to others why something is the way it is, your problems will be solved, and you won't have to worry about it ever again.

Wrong.

Instead of a **F.R.O.G.** refusing other's garbage, you become a **H.O.P.P.E.R.** (**H**oping **O**ur **P**roblems **P**romptly **E**xit **R**outinely). A **H.O.P.P.E.R.** doesn't care if someone else fixes the problem, or if they have to take matters into their own hands. They just keep bouncing into that hurdle life has thrown at them head-on, thinking it will give up and all will go smoothly. The problem is, it's not a terribly logical nor rational approach. You effectively become your own **S.T.O.R.K.** trying to fight a whole flock of other **S.T.O.R.K.**s. And you know what they say…birds of a feather flock together. Instead of clearing them out, you're just inviting more into your path.

That's what I was doing.

I would work twice as hard for twice as long.

I'd tell my colleagues the logic the owner was using in making the decision to have me in both places.

I'd charm them with my personality and high energy.

I'd make everyone like me, and all my problems would go away.

I think you already know how well that plan worked out.

But even when we know that's not how it works, it doesn't stop us from doing it.

At one point, exhausted and frustrated, I finally sat down and had a candid conversation with Howard (my Program Director). I asked what I had to do to finally earn acceptance and respect from those around me.

He said, "Sheral, are you a morning drive co-host or are you a midday talent? You can't be both. You aren't doing yourself any favors trying to be everything to everybody. Pick one and stick with it. And when you pick it, you better not have any doubts about it."

Howard had a way of saying things and telling stories that made you discover your own answers to your questions. He knew the answers. He knew YOU knew the answers. He just had to make sure you knew how to get to the answers you already had.

After a minute or two, I looked at him and said, "I'm a morning show co-host. I'm not a midday talent. I'm also not a sidekick. They might not have seen it across the street, but I know I'm what you need here."

"I'm glad you finally figured it out."

"Once I get rolling and do well, maybe everyone will relax a bit, I'll finally be part of the team, and we'll all get along better."

"Maybe, but I doubt it."

I remember being dumbfounded by his response. It took me a minute to compose myself enough to ask him why he doubted it. Why, if I did everything right, would I not be accepted as part of the team?

This would be the first time in my adult life where *"The Power of a 5 Minute Conversation"* would impact me profoundly. Words that are said so casually by others that they might not even remember saying them. Words that have the power to change your life.

I can still picture him as if he's sitting here right next to me now. He took a long drag from his cigarette and looked up at the ceiling thoughtfully (yes…they still smoked indoors then despite my constant complaints. At least they had the "lounge" next to an open door leading outside). He said, "Sheral, you aren't old enough nor experienced enough to understand who or what you are yet, so I'm going to explain it. You are what I was back when I was young. We are hired gunslingers, brought in to win the fight and take out anyone standing in our way. We aren't here because they like us or want to be our friends. We're here because of what we can do. Your weapon is your ability to read people and connect with them. That's what they need you for. That's what you're meant to do. Remember that and use it for the right reasons. If you do, you'll always land on your feet."

I didn't fully grasp what he meant back then. I thought he meant the ability to read my colleagues and my competition. That so long as I paid attention, learned quickly, worked hard, and did the job I was hired to do, everything would go well for me.

I wouldn't learn what he really meant until almost a decade later. And I would have to go full circle to discover it.

The biggest lesson to take away from this is that sometimes, it isn't the loudest **C.R.O.A.K.** or the biggest **L.E.A.P.** that gets you over the hurdle and past the **S.T.O.R.K.**.s. Sometimes, the best way to get there is to really focus on being your own **F.R.O.G.** and knowing you're doing exactly what's right for you and your path. You are the king or queen of your lily pad, and it doesn't matter how many ripples surround it. You can **REFUSE OTHER'S GARBAGE** without setting it on fire. Honestly, who benefits from a dumpster fire anyway?

CHAPTER 7

WHEN YOU BECOME YOUR OWN WORST S.T.O.R.K.

You will have amazing runs during your life where it feels like some higher power has smiled upon you and decided you DO get to live out the "happily ever after" ending of your own fairy tale.

You'll get comfortable. You'll get complacent. You might even get cocky.

And you'll never see it coming.

That moment when yet another **S.T.O.R.K.** flies in to eat you. But this time it brings a bunch of friends in and declares you to be an all-you-can-eat buffet.

But that head-honcho, leader of all these other **S.T.O.R.K.**s that descend upon you?

You'll see it when you look in the mirror. That **S.T.O.R.K.** is you.

That's what happened in my case after declaring I was the right choice for the morning show.

I stepped into my spotlight and magical things began to happen.

Not only did the show do well, but my partner and I beat the morning show I had been fired from to take the #1 position. In fact, the station overall became #1 in the market after the changes had been made. It was the first time in the station's history to beat the other one and go #1, and the first time anyone had beaten the other morning team. I still have that newspaper article. I held on to it like a priceless treasure. The station owner joked about sending my old boss a "Get Well Soon" card.

I started getting more live broadcast opportunities. I was being asked to be the voice for various commercials.

I was having the time of my life with my colleagues and riding the wave of success.

Then my husband and I discovered we were expecting our first child.

Everything…EVERYTHING felt like a charmed life. I was Cinderella at the ball.

And then life came strolling back in and chucked Cinderella's pumpkin straight at my head.

Chris was still active duty and at the mercy of the Department of Defense. That meant I was too if I wanted to keep our family together.

Four months after our daughter was born, we had just come back from an anniversary weekend in New Orleans. We had a voicemail waiting for us. Big changes were on the horizon.

Chris had a squadron commander at the time who was, shall we say, a bit of a jerk with a wandering eye. An eye that happened to spend more time looking down the shirts of other women, including my own. I made the mistake of calling him on it about the time I learned I was pregnant. Strike one.

The squadron commander's wife decided that all wives in the squadron would show up on a Saturday to bake cookies for the police on base and deliver them. She gave about 2 weeks' notice and made it mandatory. I told her I wouldn't be coming as I had two live broadcasts I was scheduled for with the station. I had work commitments. She informed me my commitments and responsibilities were to my husband's squadron. I needed to cancel my work conflicts. I told her the only responsibilities I had were to God, my family, and myself. Unless she wanted to pay me for the broadcasts, I wasn't coming. She told me if I didn't show, there would be a price to pay. I didn't show up. Strike two.

A few months later, some of the other wives in the squadron (the rebellious types like me), thought it would be fun to plan a casual dinner/ get-together on base at the club. We were having it catered, planning music, and looking to hold it as an appreciation for all the hard work everyone had been putting in. The squadron commander and his wife caught wind of it and hijacked it. They turned it into a full-blown formal affair for the arrival of the Chief of Staff for the Air Force. What was supposed to be for our group turned into a takeover for the entire base. We were all disgusted by the total disregard shown to us and my friends were on the hook to help with it. Instead of putting in the work herself, the commander's wife used her "position" to steal someone else's planning and efforts…and then took the credit for it! I did the only thing that seemed right to show my displeasure. The day of the event, I dyed my hair bright red (I'm naturally blonde), got myself a fake nose-ring, and a temporary tattoo. While I couldn't hide the hair, I could wait to spring the rest of the accessories. I wore a cashmere wrap to hide the tattoo I had strategically placed in my cleavage. I wanted to make certain the squadron commander had a place to focus his eyes when he inevitably stared at my chest again.

Dinner went as expected. Boring. Full of pomp and circumstance. Everyone was miserable at an event full of forced fun. While Chris was a bit taken aback by my new hair color, he didn't really suspect any other shenanigans. After all, I was 6 months pregnant and in formal wear. What could I really do?

These formal dinners had something called a "receiving line" where we would all parade in front of the celebrated dignitary, shake his/her hand while introducing ourselves. We would pretend we cared, they would pretend to care back, names would be forgotten instantaneously, we would be expected to butt-kiss the commanding officer and his wife over the wonderful event-planning, then go back to our seats to finish the evening.

The other wives were in on my plan. Just prior to the start of the receiving line, we excused ourselves to head to the ladies' room where they "assisted" me in placing the temporary tattoo and attaching the fake nose ring. I made certain to keep the wrap on and stay on the side of Chris where he would not notice the ring until it was too late.

We stood in the receiving line, and just as we got to the General, the commander, and his wife, I let the wrap drop. It wasn't the only thing that dropped. Jaws, silverware, belly laughs, eyes…they all dropped.

I will give the General and his wife a lot of credit. They both smiled and welcomed me warmly. Asked Chris and I when we were expecting the baby, if it was our first, etc. The commander and his wife weren't quite as cordial. Chris wasn't terribly impressed either. Strike three. This one was firmly on me. If given the chance to go back, I know for a fact I'd do it again. Not because I think what I did was the right thing (although it makes for a great story now). But because if I hadn't done it, I likely wouldn't have learned the lessons that have made me who I am today. I wouldn't be writing any of this to prevent you from making some of the same mistakes I made.

What I did was launch an over-the-top war on those I thought had wronged me.

What I DIDN'T do was think about the possible ramifications for that spectacle. All I could think was, "what could they possibly do to me?" It wouldn't take me very long to find out.

Daring life to throw hurdles at you is likely the dumbest thing you can do.

In less than a year they would transfer Chris to a base in the middle of Missouri for a non-flying position.

They were sending an up-and-coming pilot there to kill his career.

But it wasn't just to kill his career.

It would kill my career as well.

It would change everything.

There's an incredibly important lesson to be learned from this; one I wish I had learned much sooner.

In our quest to stop letting people and situations hold us back, we start seeing EVERYTHING as a hurdle except ourselves. We become so focused on what's coming at us from around every corner that we become blind to what's happening from within. We sabotage our own success.

I thought I was putting a stop to things and people that could take my joy and success away from me. I was fighting to keep everything I had worked to get. But that became my only focus…the fight.

Had I not been my own **S.T.O.R.K.**, I'd have looked at things with **RATIONAL KNOWLEDGE** and understood that there are more ways to set boundaries and **REFUSE OTHERS' GARBAGE** than by launching a full-on assault. I could have been far more diplomatic and tactful than I had been. I didn't have to one-up the obnoxious behavior.

Plus, fighting eats up so much of your time, energy, and joy. I know this from years of experience. Before you go crashing through the hurdle, take a deep breath, and look at your options. You might find you can just as easily go around it or gently move it out of your path instead of trying to destroy it. You'll find you get the same results, without the bruises and injuries.

CHAPTER 8

SWIMMING WITH YOUR INNER DEMONS

In January of 1995 we said goodbye to everything we had come to know and love- careers, friends, our home- and moved ourselves to a 5-acre box in the middle of Missouri.

I was in my mid-20s and faced with a 9-month-old (who was probably the easiest baby in the world…thank God), a husband who was a professional pilot but would no longer be flying, undiagnosed post-partum depression, no family or friends close by, no support, and a cold-turkey ending to my childhood dream of being a radio "star."

Being young with limited life experience is difficult enough. Being any age and trying to tackle one of those hurdles is a struggle that many have trouble getting over.

Handling them all at one time and trying to do it by yourself is a recipe for failure of epic proportions.

Chris would go to work early and come home late. When he did come home, he wouldn't talk much. He would isolate himself and spend his hours on his computer. He hated his job and was resigned to rotting away for years in the cellars of the Air Force base until they finally decided they had no use for him.

I don't blame him for not wanting to interact. I was a mess. As I look back, I don't even recognize the person I had become.

I spent most of my days going through the motions of motherhood. She was my joy and happiness, and I couldn't even appreciate it or feel it because I was so caught up in a pit of depression.

I cried almost all the time. I didn't have anyone to talk to. I didn't have a purpose. And it was amplified by severe post-partum depression and extreme hormonal imbalances that weren't then diagnosed. I didn't even know I had a problem that could have been corrected. Instead, I was told by family and friends who weren't there to "be an adult and handle the situation." I needed to "get over" feeling sorry for myself and act like a grown-up.

Chris thought it might be good to find a job and get in-volved outside the home again. It sounded like a solid solu-tion. I took a position with the local university at their public radio station. I was brought on to interpret the Arbitron rat-ings books and devise a plan to make their station competitive against the Kansas City commercial stations. I was also sup-posed to train their students to compete with seasoned on-air professionals in the Kansas City market, as well as deliver a modernized, updated show of my own to the local market.

As I look back, I never should have even considered that position. There was no way to succeed.

For starters, only the smallest sliver of their listening area overlapped the Kansas City market. There was absolutely no way to compete in that market unless you moved the station or doubled the signal. Neither of those things were happening.

Secondly, public radio stations by their very nature aren't designed to be like commercial radio stations. If they were, they'd have COMMERCIALS paying advertising revenue for airtime rather than sponsors and donation mentions.

Thirdly, you can't expect some 19-year-old student who has no real interest in pursuing a radio career to compete with a radio professional. Not everyone has the talent and drive to be a radio personality. PERSONALITY is what makes or breaks an individual who wants to be an on-air talent. That's not something you can teach. You can hone their personality and customize techniques to improve their delivery, but it isn't something you can use a standard template to teach. That was something that fell on deaf ears. My "instruction and training" was supposed to align with the textbook teachings of the University's Broadcasting courses. I have yet to meet a textbook student who ever had any true success on-air in any major market. The textbook-taught "radio star" is much like Bigfoot, aliens, or a unicorn. I'm sure they're out there, but I've never met them.

Finally, they had no idea who their ideal target audience was. They wanted to appeal to a younger crowd like their students while still being accepted and listened to by the surrounding farming community. The best way I could explain this is if you tried to create a place that made big-game hunters and members of PETA feel equally happy. You can't put out a content-driven product that has great appeal to two groups that are completely on opposite ends of the spectrum. The local community (most of the listening audience), wanted to hear news, weather (including sustained winds), and grain prices. Students wanted edgy music, concert news, and ideas for what to do on the weekend. To think you can please everyone like that is a lesson in both futility and insanity. Sadly, I was so desperate to get back into the industry that I decided I was the miracle-worker who could accomplish it.

It lasted 4 months before I couldn't stand it anymore. I found a part-time position at a commercial radio station in Kansas City an hour away (more weekend work and commercial production) and decided I would do exactly what I had done back in Louisiana. It was only a matter of time before I was back on top of my game. Or so I thought.

I spent 3 years driving an hour one way to do weekend shows, filling in periodically during the week for a full-timer, and doing production here and there. I was told I likely wouldn't ever be offered a full-time position because I lived so far away. During the weekdays when I was home, I found myself searching for something…anything…to chase away the failures I was facing.

My marriage had fallen apart.

Motherhood didn't come naturally to me. I made sure Devon had everything she needed, but I wasn't dialed in at all. I tried to be the best Mom I knew how to be, but I wasn't very good at it. I don't think I gave her the proper emotional nurturing she needed because I didn't even have enough to give myself.

I was going nowhere fast with my career.

I couldn't even head back to Louisiana to do my old show…my partner had recently passed away after losing his battle to cancer.

I had surrounded myself with "friends" who were just as miserable as I was; spending days drinking to excess or dabbling in recreational drugs.

I wanted to die.

All before the age of 30.

3 years of a destructive wash, rinse, repeat cycle before I woke up hung over one day, looked out the window while making my daughter's breakfast and saw my reflection in the glass.

That was the day I decided I couldn't do it anymore. I couldn't do it to her. I couldn't do it to me.

I filed for divorce and started looking for houses closer to the radio station in Kansas City.

I had no idea how I was going to do this, but I knew I wouldn't live long if I didn't make a clean break.

I found a house in an older neighborhood about 30 minutes from the radio station. I was offered a full-time position as a Production Assistant for the 8-station cluster.

I straightened myself out, poured myself into Devon, made new friends (those who weren't on a path to self-destruction), adopted a dog, and started counseling.

When I didn't have Devon, I either worked late hours at the station or spent late nights with friends because I couldn't stand the thought of being alone.

I didn't date. I didn't want to. The last thing I needed was another relationship when I didn't even have a good relationship with myself.

At the age of 30, I realized:

I had never been alone.

I had never had to work at being successful.

I had never figured out what my real purpose in life was supposed to be.

I had never become comfortable in my own skin.

I had never learned how to properly ask for help.

The word "amphibian" is derived from a couple of Greek words meaning "both kinds of life." It's when you're able to transform from one life to another, but still manage to exist in both places.

As I look back, this is the part of my life where I began to truly transition from tadpole (basically a **F.I.S.H.**) to an actual **F.R.O.G.** I had to learn how to be okay being on my own and learn how to survive and thrive before I could be any good to anyone else in either a personal or professional manner. With the counseling, support of my family and friends, and a desire to provide a stable life for both my daughter and I:

I became a better mother.

I became a better friend.

I became more determined to put in the work, climb the ladder, and succeed professionally.

I learned how to ask others for help frequently. I think that was the hardest one. I was always so embarrassed by what I didn't know, what I couldn't do, lack of finances, lack of awareness, etc.

I learned that mental health is every bit as important as physical health…and it isn't something to be shunned or avoided. Face it head on. Admit it. Work to fix it every day.

I wasn't perfect. I wasn't even close. But I was better than I was, improving daily, and looking forward to the progress.

There are no deep, philosophical lessons to be learned from this chapter in my life, except that learning to like your own company is important to your overall well-being. If you find yourself struggling and trying to get through it all alone, I hope you'll take what I'm going to say next to heart.

Depression is real and debilitating. It doesn't go away if you ignore it. It is an illness. Let's take diabetes as an example. You get an exercise and a nutrition plan, even medications to prevent it from destroying your life. Depression should be treated the same way. It's not something you just "get over." If you are having issues that last more than a few days, see a professional to help you come up with the best plan for YOU. There is ZERO shame in it, and you are not alone.

It doesn't matter what is causing it. What matters is that you take the steps to treat it. You might not see it or feel it at the time, but you matter to someone. Likely a lot of "someones." You are important enough to be helped. In time, you'll see it too.

CHAPTER 9

THE F.I.S.H. AND S.T.O.R.K. CONNECTION

Work and repair.

That was the theme over the next 3½ years.

There were a lot of nights spent crying. A lot of days spent worrying about finances. Every day trying to be better for myself and for my daughter.

As each day passed it got easier. My confidence and skills improved both at work and at home. I was comfortable enough in my space to push for bigger and better things.

Comfort. That's an interesting word. We strive to be comfortable, but it's when we think we finally have it that the hurdles start cropping up again and we find ourselves surrounded by a full platoon of **S.T.O.R.K**.s.

2½ years had gone by at the radio cluster. I had worked my tail off trying to prove myself. I was getting character feature opportunities on a couple of the morning shows. My voice was on commercials all over the city. Yet when I applied for on-air positions, I wasn't even considered. When I discussed the possibility of a raise with my supervisor, I was told upper management wouldn't approve it…it wasn't in the budget.

Friends, if something smells **F.I.S.H.**y, chances are there's either a **F.I.S.H.** nearby, or a **S.T.O.R.K.** feasting on them. And sometimes they are one in the same. Follow your nose!

While learning to repair myself and ask others for help, I had to learn to trust. That wasn't an easy task given my family upbringing, nor my past career experiences. What I failed to learn was to not just trust, but to VERIFY as well. Not everyone is your friend through thick and thin, and not everyone has your best interests at heart.

Loyalty is something that plays a huge role in my world. I am loyal to a fault, and that fault was about to expose itself.

The General Manager for the radio station who had hired me originally to do part-time had an on-air opening. More of a transitional day-part opening. It would require me to be gone two hours of each day from my production assistant duties…mostly over the lunch hour. I was ecstatic to get back to a regular on-air gig, and not just something part-time on the weekends. I asked if someone would be helping my Production Supervisor since I didn't want to leave him in the lurch. The GM laughed and said, "I don't think you need to worry about your loyalties to him. He certainly isn't worried about his loyalty to you." It wouldn't take more than a week to discover what he meant.

My supervisor was livid. How could I just up and leave the department? Did I understand the strain it would put upon him? I didn't understand what sort of strain he could be imagining. It was two hours…during his lunch hour (his lunches tended to go long) …and I was STILL going to be handling my share of the commercial production. The only imposition it would be is if a client needed to do a recording session (which was a rarity during those hours) or if a commercial needed to be done asap for a quick turn. But there were other people that could cover that if he was gone.

It didn't matter. I had somehow betrayed him. He wouldn't even speak to me for a couple of weeks afterward.

To further show his displeasure, he started adding late recording sessions and extra production to my load. It didn't matter that I had to pick up my daughter from daycare by a certain time. I couldn't understand why he had turned so ugly. This wasn't behavior I was accustomed to seeing from him.

Then came the eye-opener. I was brought back to discuss a salary increase with upper management since I was adding additional responsibilities to my job description. The Director of Sales was handling it, and he looked uncomfortable and embarrassed. He asked me why I had never asked for a raise over and above the probationary salary they had started me at.

I just looked at him as if he had spoken to me in a foreign language. Probationary salary??? I hadn't been aware that it WAS a probationary salary…one that was to have been increased after the first 3 months of my employment. I had been there going on 3 years.

I explained that I had made several inquiries about a salary increase but was told that it was denied each time my supervisor had presented it. It turned out my requests had never been presented. Not once. But my supervisor had given himself annual increases without hesitation. My salary was increased substantially, and I moved on to my new responsibilities.

I would come to learn that not only had he taken credit for, and rewarded himself, for all the work I had been doing, but he had actively gone out of his way to sabotage any attempts I had made to get back into an on-air position, mostly because HE wanted to go back on the air.

This is a lesson most of us will learn the hard way, and some of us never learn it at all. Not everyone is deserving of your loyalty, nor your trust. But not everyone is worthy of you coming at them with barrels blazing either. I could have gone the route of getting even and trying to sabotage him as well, but what good would that have done? It just would have been a constant negative escalation. It was more stress and drama than I needed. And I had just finished learning my lesson regarding petty fighting. It's what landed me in Missouri in the first place. Better to just swallow that pill and move forward.

Was my supervisor a hurdle in my path? Yes. He was a **F.I.S.H.** who was struggling to find a way out of his own situation. I was a threat to that. When a **F.I.S.H.** feels threatened, sometimes they lash out and become a **S.T.O.R.K.** to the person they see as the obstacle in their way. That's what was happening here.

But I hadn't considered I was the same to him. I had become a full-blown **S.T.O.R.K.** in his eyes, and he was lashing out at me irrationally. At least I hope he was being irrational. If he truly was that big of a jerk…well…I'll save my speculation and thoughts on that for another time.

Remember how I stated early in the first few chapters that to get over a hurdle you need to **L.E.A.P.**? I hadn't done that here. I hadn't **LOOKED** nor **LISTENED**. I hadn't **EDUCATED** myself to what was happening around me. I didn't **ACT** by going to upper management and advocating for myself. I never asked why I was being looked over for raises and advancement opportunities.

Getting over life's hurdles isn't always accomplished by focusing on yourself. Sometimes it's a matter of paying attention to others and their own struggles so you don't trip over their hurdles while you're trying to get to your own finish line. My eyes were wide open now.

The on-air position didn't last long. It's much easier to find someone to fill a daytime slot than it is to find someone with the proper skill set willing to do only production; and not for the salary they were paying me. I don't know the exact reasoning, but it didn't matter. I wasn't being fired. I was just going back to my old position.

But there was no going back at that point. I was ready to move forward, and I couldn't do that had I stayed there. You can't do great things in an environment where there is no trust. It's not good for anyone, and I had just finished putting myself back together. I didn't want to jeopardize that.

Chris and I had begun dating again. I had a solid and supportive group of friends. I didn't need to prove myself any longer.

So, I gave my two weeks' notice for my full-time production position, took a part-time/fill-in position with a local country station being run by a Hall of Fame Program Director, and "put the band back together" with Chris. We remarried, bought a new house, "added a keyboard player" (a new baby on the way), and I looked forward to a fresh start.

What were my take-aways (besides marrying the same guy twice would make for interesting stories)?

    1. Trust, but verify. Not everyone is out to get you. Not everyone is your friend. There will be times

and circumstances where a person you thought was your friend will be out to get you, and times when your enemy becomes your advocate. Sometimes that person will be you.

2. You aren't always the good guy in someone else's story. Pay attention to those around you and their motivations. You can't always avoid the situations, but at least you won't play into them and make the situation worse for yourself. The goal is to get past the hurdle, not try to destroy it or go into battle with it.

3. When you cannot change a situation, know that it is acceptable to walk away from it completely. One of the ways to get to your ultimate finish-line might involve choosing a brand-new path. You may find some unexpected rewards and joys along the way, too.

CHAPTER 10

HISTORY WILL REPEAT ITSELF IF YOU LET IT

When you have unfinished business and haven't learned the lessons "The Universe" wants you to figure out, you get thrown into Deja vu situations to see if you handle them differently this time around. You're doomed to keep repeating them if you don't.

My world had become much simpler and far more satisfying.

Chris and I had remarried, sold both of our houses, and bought a new one to give us a fresh start. Baby #2 was on the way. My days were spent hiking lake trails with the dogs, watching Devon play, and visiting with the neighbors. I still filled in at the country station from time to time to feed my creative itch. We planned for Chris to retire from the Air Force, pick up a pilot slot with an airline, and settle into civilian suburban life. All we needed was the white picket fence.

The second Gulf War and 9-11 happened months before Chris was going to put in for retirement. The airline jobs dried up. It was decided he wouldn't retire after all. But that also meant that it was time for us to be transferred. They weren't going to let us stay in Missouri.

We were allowed to rank the choices we were given: Hawaii, Virginia…even Nebraska would have been okay. At least with Omaha, we would have been able to visit friends with a few hours of drive time. We submitted our picks and waited to see where we would end up.

We were incredibly shocked and more than a little dismayed to learn we were being sent back to Louisiana. Come on! Not even Nebraska? It hadn't even been on our list. Not because it was a horrible place to be. It wasn't, and we still had friends there. Our reasons for being upset came mostly out of concern for Devon's schooling and a strong distaste in our mouths due to our career experiences there. We packed up our daughters (aged 8 years and 6 weeks), the dog, the cats, and our happy home. Then we braced ourselves for what the next 3 years might present.

One of the first things I did after arriving was reach out to my old radio friends. I wasn't interested in getting back into radio, but I wanted to make certain I had a circle of people around me that was supportive. I didn't want to fall back into the destructive and depressive slump I had fallen into when I had moved away the last time.

Much had changed. It wasn't a mom-and-pop radio landscape any longer. Everything was owned by corporate radio and many of the stations that had been competitors before I left were now housed under the same roof. One of those stations was the first station I had worked for. That meant that I would likely run into my original morning show partner while visiting some of my former colleagues from the other station.

I decided the past was the past and happily visited with everyone, including the original co-host. It was fun trading stories about the changes we had all gone through over the years within the industry. I had grown up both personally and professionally. They all noticed it. When I said goodbye for the day, I knew it would be a matter of time before I was back in the thick of it. I just didn't know when or how. As it turns out, it would be approximately 72 hours. The radio industry is addictive and hard to walk away from.

I remember it vividly. I was unpacking dishes and trying to figure out where half of our things were when the caller ID flashed showing the radio station's number.

On the other end was a very friendly, laid-back voice with a Tennessee drawl. It was the new Program Director at the country station I had worked for in Shreveport. The station that had left such a bad taste in my mouth. The station where my former co-host was still working.

Les had heard "through the grapevine" that I had morning show experience in the market, that I had large market experience in Kansas City (#29 radio market in the U.S. as opposed to Shreveport, ranked #131), and that I might be interested in finding an on-air position here in town. I told him I was open to discussing it but had only just moved back. I hadn't unpacked anything and didn't even know where any of my old air-check tapes were. Heck, I hadn't been in town two weeks yet.

We talked for a bit, and he learned that I had worked for a buddy of his…the Hall of Fame Program Director (Ted) at the country station in Kansas City I had just left. We agreed to meet in person a few days later to discuss what sort of opportunities might be available in the future.

Ironically, we both called Ted in Kansas City to vet each other prior to our meeting. I can't thank him enough for giving me his seal of approval to Les. Les would also go on to become a Hall of Fame Program Director and was one of the main reasons Kenny Chesney got mainstream exposure. He was a bit of an unconventional champion for those who didn't quite fit into the boxes laid out for us, and for some unknown reason, he saw something in me he thought could work.

The current female co-host wasn't a good fit in their morning show. She was young, not from the area originally, and was having difficulty meshing with my former partner. He had gone to Les, and they agreed it would be best to find someone to take her place (hmmmm…does that sound just a little bit familiar???) and they thought that person might be me.

I wasn't interested in doing that to someone else. While my situation had been a bit different with the harassment, I still remembered how it felt to be let go and finding out there had been a plan in place to replace me happening behind my back. It stung, and I didn't want to be the cause for someone else to feel that way. I wanted to be up front and open about things.

Les had assured me that she knew her position was on the line based on the ratings, and that they would be offering her a position in the Promotions department, as she was quite skilled and organized in that field. And it would only happen if the ratings in the next book came back weak. That would happen within the month.

I told him I would need to think about it.

The Arbitron ratings came back, and they weren't good. Honestly, I hadn't realized how much the station had dropped in the market share. They weren't the powerhouse I remembered from when I was there the first time around. The decision had been made. They were going to let her go. I still wasn't the official pick to replace her. They wanted to hear how I sounded on-air and see how I carried myself with a co-host. They wanted me to do a live audition. Like I said earlier, Deja vu. I'd already seen this movie once before.

They didn't want to tip anyone off that I was being looked at as the new morning co-host on the country station, so they set me up with the co-host of their Hit Music/Pop station. The female co-host was on vacation for a week, and I would be there under the premise of filling in as a guest host while she was gone. I already knew I was going to get the gig. There wasn't an ounce of doubt in my mind. The only doubt I had was whether it was the right thing to do.

I tracked down my old Program Director Howard. He agreed to meet me for lunch, catch up, and offer his sage advice.

We chatted about my time in Kansas City, how much everything had changed in the industry and in Shreveport/Bossier City in general, the kids, his health, and everything in between. Then we moved from the small talk to my concerns about taking a morning show at the other company. I even asked if a position was available within the company he was at.

He explained that there wasn't anything that would ever be worth really going after in the company he was with because corporate radio had moved in with a vengeance. My best opportunities would be with the other company.

He told me it was foolish of me to worry about the other gal. I hadn't done anything to get her fired from her position.

That decision had likely been made before the ratings had even come back, and before they even realized I was back in town. He also assured me that he had heard good things about Les. He was a decent guy with tons of radio knowledge.

Then came the advice that only Howard could give. He said, *"You understand it now, don't you? You understand that you're a gunslinger. I see it more now since you've been gone. When you walk into a room you don't have to even speak. But people know. They know it across the street…that's why they want you. You know it too now, don't you?"*

"Yeah, I have a pretty good idea of what you were talking about now."

"If you already know the answer, why are you here with me? It can't be because of my charming personality and a desire to watch me smoke myself to death."

"Once I give them what they need…and I know that I will…what do I need to do when they decide to turn on me? Because we both know once they get what they want, my honeymoon will be over."

He didn't laugh. He didn't crack a smile. He ordered two pieces of pie, two more refills of coffee, and then looked at me.

"Of course, they're going to come after you, and this time they're going to go after you harder than before. But why do you care? It's not about them. You need to do this for you. So, I'm going to give you my final bit of advice.

1. *Trust your instinct and do what you do best. When they try to make you question yourself, double down and do it even harder.*

2. *They will try to take credit for what you do. Let them only up to a certain point. You know what you bring to the table. Make sure they do too.*

3. *Keep your head on a swivel and grow eyes in the back of your head. Keep your ears listening at all times. When the knives come out, at least you'll see it coming.*

4. *When they try to screw you over (and they will), hold your ground and don't cave in. You know what's right and wrong, what's fair and what isn't. Make sure they know you know it too.*

5. *At some point you will know when it's no longer worth the fight. When that day comes, leave on your terms; not theirs.*

6. *Enjoy every minute of the ride while it lasts. When it's finished, make sure you have no regrets and no unfinished business.*

7. *Order the pie. Always order the pie."*

It would be a short hour and the last real conversation we would ever have. It was meaningful nevertheless, as it typically was with him. I only hope he knew how much I liked and respected him. I suspect he did. I wish I had told him more often. That would be my only regret where he was concerned. That and my inability to convince him to quit smoking. He passed away from lung cancer in 2009.

The week of the live audition/fill-in came, and it felt like home again. It was fun, it was entertaining and filled with laughs. The co-host of the show and I may or may not be responsible for causing the death of singer Robert Palmer (he had a heart attack weeks after we tried to set him up on a blind date with our receptionist and queried him about selling out to a fish stick company. Coincidence? Perhaps).

It felt like we had been doing the show together for years instead of having just met on day one of my audition. And it wasn't even the show I was auditioning for. At least I didn't think it was. Turns out there was a fight over which station would get me. Les and the country station won. They offered me the position, I took it, and I would go on the air officially in a couple of weeks' time. In the meantime, they would have me "sneak" in to get familiar with the studio and production equipment by coming in a few times a week at random times. They thought it would prevent anyone from becoming suspicious of me being around. It was the most ridiculous thing I had ever heard. It was a building with 3 stations in it. Radio stations where people talk and notice everything. Keeping a secret there was as effective as telling my brother not to tell someone what they were getting for Christmas - there was no chance.

Sure enough, the morning co-host I was replacing found out. She didn't accept the promotional position she was offered. She also didn't have many kind words for me.

The co-host from the other show who came back from vacation to discover I was back and had filled in while she was away? She found out her position had been in jeopardy as well. The irony? It was the same co-host I had replaced when I had worked for Howard. You can imagine how well that went over. I hadn't even known it was on the table, yet somehow, I was to blame. We never would become friendly with one another. Some things are just not meant to be.

There was one secret that had been kept, however. They weren't just looking to replace the female co-host on the country station. They were also replacing my old co-host. He didn't know it, but they were actively searching for someone to take his place. They wanted a fresh, new morning team.

I found out two days before he was gone. He insisted I had known and went behind his back to get him fired. Of course, he would think that. After all, it's what he would have done. In fact, it's what he HAD done to me years before. There was no point trying to explain myself or convince him otherwise. It wouldn't change anything. I had a job to do, and I suddenly had to do it alone until they could find a suitable partner.

Finding a suitable partner would become a challenge all unto itself. The first one came in for the interview and I knew immediately it wasn't going to work. Bit of a chauvinistic snob. Old school. Looked at the female as a sidekick. We met and immediately disliked each other. Not just mildly, but a rival gang sort of dislike for one another. Les pulled me aside to ask what I thought of him, and I told him in a less than diplomatic sort of way. He just laughed and said that the friction can make for a great show sometimes. He was going to hire him. My only question at that point was if they intended to have me step back and behave like a sidekick. I was already a month into the show by myself and building a following. I had created a "Sher on the air and everywhere" persona that was starting to catch on. I needed an honest answer about what their intentions were for the show.

Les was always a bit worried about me being tough to keep under control, but he also recognized my talent, and did everything in his power to showcase it to let both me, and the station, shine. He didn't care if you were male or female. Talent was talent, and he wanted me at full throttle. He promised me I would never be less than the equal co-host he had hired me to be. I believed him. He had been honest with me from the moment I had met him. He knew that so long as he told me what was going on, I would stay loyal. The only thing I wouldn't suffer is being lied to or betrayed. He wasn't known to do either, and I would come to trust and adore him as if he were my radio dad.

I wouldn't have to worry about the new partner. He decided to renege on the deal the day he was supposed to arrive. I won't lie. I wasn't sad about it.

They brought in the midday guy as a temporary fill-in so I would have someone to interact with on the show. He was a good kid. Talented. Not morning show material, but he could have been trained to be in time. He was a terrific producer and, ironically, a great sidekick. I decided I would do something that was pretty much unheard of. I'd make it MY show. A morning show on a country format where the so-called "star" was a woman. I would become my own Wolfman Jack. Coincidental, given he had created his persona in Shreveport. Now I would do the same.

By the time they found a partner for me, I had already started a slow build with the rating trends. But this partner was perfect. He not only wanted me to be an equal partner but felt the success of the show would rely on our ability to showcase my personality. He was smart, creative, laid-back, and had an infectious laugh. He and the show would be what held me together for the next 3 months.

About the time they hired on Dave, Chris got orders he was being deployed to Qatar. We had only been there a couple of months, hadn't even sold our house back in Missouri yet, and they were sending him to the Middle East. I would have to handle everything without him. Two young girls, a new job with long hours and multiple live appearances, real estate sales, finances…everything. On top of that, I was noticing developmental issues with our youngest Katy. She didn't laugh and coo like other babies. She would get over-stimulated with ease. She wouldn't sleep unless someone would hold her. And it wasn't just fussy baby stuff. Something wasn't right. I just couldn't put a finger on it. And I wouldn't have time to figure it out. A nanny was hired, Chris headed overseas, the promotional blitz was on at the station, and I would literally not sleep more than 3-4 hours a night for the next 3 months. Say hello to the newest **S.T.O.R.K.!**

I would get through it, but not without cost. My relationships, family, and health would all suffer. The only thing I could focus on was the show. I didn't have the energy for anything else. Rationally I should have invested that energy into my health and my family, but that's the funny thing about a **S.T.O.R.K.;** they **TAKE OUR RATIONAL KNOWLEDGE.**

By the time Chris came back home, I was close to a nervous breakdown. I was on to the second nanny and sleep deprivation had left me feeling manic.

My partner Dave left after management chose not to honor their agreement regarding his housing. He had been living in a hotel room during the week and driving back to his wife and daughter two hours away in Dallas each weekend. He had finally had enough. Once again, I found myself without a partner.

To add insult to injury, I got a tattoo during that time. I'm not sure why I thought it was a good idea. It's a horribly ugly tattoo that I keep to this day to remind me to take better care of myself and get enough sleep. A permanent reminder about the consequences of irrational decisions. A permanent reminder about what should be a priority in life (this wasn't one that should have ever been a priority, trust me).

In case you're wondering what makes it such a horrible tattoo, let me just say that it looks like a portion of a man's anatomy. Yes, THAT portion. Except it looks like the world's tiniest and angriest example. I have won contests for the ugliest tattoo because of it. But it isn't supposed to be a male anatomical piece…it's a frog. A poison dart frog. A terrible expression of a poison dart frog. Despite the lack of artistic integrity, I'm certain that my choice of the poison dart frog was the universe or God trying to teach me about *being* a **F.R.O.G.** long before I would understand what it really meant. Maybe I missed the memo because it was such an awful rendition.

But I had made it. I managed to get the house sold in Missouri. I kept the household afloat (just barely). I had built the foundation for a successful show and would somehow manage to continue that growth despite being without a partner once again. And I would finally sleep. Everything would be better once I got some sleep.

I was stronger than I had thought I would be. I wasn't given much of a choice. I guess everything could have fallen apart, but my survival instinct had kicked in as flawed as it was. I credit the growth I experienced during the time I was divorced for getting me through this situation. It's amazing what we can accomplish when we build upon our past experiences. People need to give themselves more credit for what they are capable of handling.

Once again, they brought in the midday guy to serve as the temporary fill-in while they searched for "another perfect partner." That poor kid. He was good enough to stand in, but they wouldn't consider him as the permanent male position on my morning show. I petitioned to have them hire him. It would be easier to find a midday person rather than another morning guy I would have chemistry with on-air. And I liked this kid. We got along well, and he was teachable. Management wouldn't entertain the idea. My temporary partner didn't think I was doing enough to get him the spot. He questioned whether I was doing anything at all. Radio is full of insecurities and paranoia. I'm of the opinion that we go into the industry rather than going to counseling. It's a place we celebrate our creative yet semi-broken personalities. I still maintain that there is more validity than kidding in that opinion.

Dave and I stayed in contact. He was actively trying to market our team for a morning show position in a bigger market. Chris and I talked and decided that if the opportunity came, we could somehow make it work being in different locations. With him being in the military, he couldn't pick up and go anywhere I might end up. It wouldn't be ideal, but we had learned after his deployment that we could handle anything. And while I loved Les and the on-air staff, I was not as impressed with management.

Hoping for a new opportunity with Dave in another market was a longshot, so I focused on the show and hoped they would never find a new partner for me. I could do this without one. The ratings numbers were slowly but steadily climbing. I didn't need a partner. I just needed consistency.

The listeners would jokingly tease me about running off partners. I'd laugh and bite my tongue. I couldn't tell them about the dirty laundry happening behind the scenes with the General Manager and General Sales Manager.

I remember one of our advertising clients from the local Nissan dealership asked how I could continue to do well going from one co-host to the other. I said something to the effect of "I'm still talking to the same person I was before. I'm not talking to a partner.

I'm talking to the mom in her car driving her kids to school.

I'm talking to the woman in her bathroom putting on her makeup before heading to work.

I'm talking to the guy who's stuck in traffic and frustrated he's going to be behind schedule all day long.

I'm talking to the guy on his business trip or farming his fields, realizing he's missing a birthday party or an anniversary.

I'm talking to that lonely person who just needs a friend they can count on to always be there. All they need to do is turn on their radio, and I'm there.

The conversation doesn't change. I just customize the flow of the message depending on the personality of whatever new co-host they put in front of me. My partners have become plug and play. The messaging is not."

That was my "a-ha" moment. It had never been about how I interacted with the people I worked with nor about the show. It was about who was tuning in. It was about the conversation with them and my ability to hear them...to listen to what THEY needed. It was about whether I could speak to them in a way that they knew I was paying attention to what they wanted. And it didn't matter what partner, sidekick, or fancy bells and whistles contest I had going. What mattered was how they felt after spending time with me.

I finally fully understood what Howard meant when he gave me his gunslinger speech:

"Your weapon is your ability to read people and connect with them. That's what they need you for. That's what you're meant to do. Remember that and use it for the right reasons. If you do, you'll always land on your feet."

Months went by and I thought management had finally given up and would let me keep the midday guy when I got the news. They wanted to hire someone and had set up dinner plans to for me to meet him and give my input. They called him…Gator.

Our dinner was an interesting one. Not in the good sort of way, either. Les couldn't make it, so our General Manager took his place. Then there was Gator.

Gator wasn't refined or polished like Dave had been. Gator was…well…Gator. He was your typical Uncle Buck showing up in his best Bob Seger t-shirt (he didn't show up in a t-shirt for the dinner, thankfully), hair a mess, 70's porno mustache proudly adorned on his face. He was a little too loud, a little too proud of some of his inappropriate jokes, but he had a warm and friendly demeanor. I wasn't sure if I should like him or not. Given my history with partners, I wasn't exactly feeling very open and trusting. It could've gone either way. It wasn't until he started discussing what he would be doing with the show to the General Manager as if I wasn't even there that I decided I didn't like him. That wasn't going to work for me. But if history was a lesson, I already knew I wouldn't have a say in it. My presence there was solely as a courtesy. Knowing what I know now about him, he would never have intentionally done anything to make me feel that way. He just didn't know the situation. But I didn't know anything about him at that time, and I wasn't having any part of it.

I sat back, ordered the most expensive steak on the menu (the GM was paying), a glass of wine, and listened to see just how bad things were going to be for me going forward if they hired this guy.

I was almost finished with my dinner before my potential partner finally asked me a question. He wanted to know why my former partner left, what I liked and disliked the most about doing the show, and if I thought I could work with him if he accepted their offer. Good questions. Better late than never, I guess. And he had just confirmed that my input hadn't mattered. They had already offered him the position. Including me in the dinner to meet him was solely for show.

Before I could answer, the GM jumped in and painted a picture of Dave in the most unflattering way possible. He didn't just spin a different opinion on the way things happened, but he flat out lied regarding a sizable portion of it. Then he had the nerve to say, "Sher is so much better off without him as a partner and will be thrilled to do a show with you."

It was too much. He could fire me at that point, but I wasn't going to let him put words in my mouth. I looked at Gator shand said, "First of all, 'Sher' doesn't need to have anyone speak for her. She speaks for herself. I'm not better off without Dave. I loved having Dave as my partner. The only reason he left is they didn't honor their contractual agreements with him. He stayed as long as he did out of respect for Les and out of both professional respect and personal friendship with me. You're being told an out and out lie about what happened and that should be concerning to you. You want to know if I think I can work with you? At this point, I could work with a small dog if they put it on the air with me. I've already done it with 4 partner changes and on my own. And the numbers keep slowly climbing. You know why? Because it's my show. Make no mistake about it. I built it. Not management, not some magical partner. I did the work and I stayed consistent. And it will remain mine until management decides it isn't. I can work with you or anybody else. But it doesn't mean I have to like you. Thank you for a most enlightening dinner. If you'll excuse me, I have a show to prep for tomorrow."

I left, unsure if I would actually have a show the next day to go to. I fully expected the GM to fire me, but I was right about what I had said, and I figured he knew I was right as well. He wouldn't like it much, but he needed me. And whether I liked Gator or not, he had a right to know the truth about everything and what he was walking into. I was tired of being lied to or watching other people being lied to. If there was a sword to fall upon, it would be this one. It would be a sword of honesty. If I got punished for this less than diplomatic boss move, so be it. At least I'd be able to look myself in the mirror afterward.

I didn't get fired but I did get chewed out by Les the next day. I can't say I didn't have it coming in some ways. He didn't need the extra stress brought on by my sassy outbursts to a potential new partner and to our boss. But like I told him, it mattered to me. It all mattered. I wasn't going to lie for management, and I wasn't going to stick around if I was being delegated to the role of a sidekick for some new guy from the swamp. Les told me I needed to trust him. He wasn't about to let anyone turn me into a sidekick, but I needed to work with him. He'd keep Gator under control. I hated the idea, but I loved Les. I agreed and Gator was hired.

It took a month or so before I started to warm up to him. Gator was sort of like a fungus. If you sat still long enough, he'd finally grow on you. And he was talented. Les was wrong about being able to control him though. Much like he couldn't quite control me. But it didn't matter. Because Gator understood that I wasn't a timid wallflower. He leaned into it, and it became OUR show. We were equals. Partners. Partners in crime in a lot of ways. We became friends, and then like family. We invited the listeners to become our friends and family. There wasn't a moment we weren't on the same page with regards to the show. And the best part was we were genuinely having fun. It had been a long time since I had loved what I was doing. This was exactly like I had pictured in my childhood dreams.

We nearly gave management a heart attack by pushing the envelope with the show. It was a country show that we treated like a rock format morning show. We played pranks, we brought in comedians and entertainers, we cut loose about everything. And it paid off in dividends. The ratings skyrocketed and we became the #1 morning show in the market by double digits.

Remember how Howard advised me to enjoy every minute of the ride while it lasted? I took it to heart on every level possible. "Sher" truly WAS everywhere! At every big event. Introducing performers on stages in front of thousands of people. Presenting the grand opening of businesses. Driving a new vehicle on loan from the Nissan dealership weekly. I was living larger than life with my face on billboards, the sides of buses, and on park benches (although the thought of someone sitting on my face was a little disturbing). I sat on expert panels at Morning Show Bootcamp, giving advice to other radio talent at conferences in New Orleans and Los Angeles. I was friends with musicians and comedians. In my own mind, I was finally starting to achieve that "Wolfman Jack" level I had dreamt of as a kid.

But every ride comes to an end eventually.

Gator and I continued to grow and stay strong, both with the ratings and as a team. We had negotiated a bonus structure if we hit certain numbers in each quarterly ratings book. We had also pushed for syndication to get our show reaching into more markets. We were a "cash cow" for the company and wanted to be rewarded for consistently performing and delivering. Management wasn't cooperative. There was always some sort of loophole as to why we weren't getting our bonuses. There was always an excuse as to why we weren't hammering out details for syndication.

I got my notification that we were coming up on contract negotiations about the time the new Arbitron ratings book came out. As I mentioned, Gator and I were crushing it in the morning timeslot with double-digit dominance in the market. Tom Joyner, Steve Harvey, Big D & Bubba- the syndicated shows couldn't touch us. No one could. At least not at that time. Not so quiet whispers in the hallways talked about how I was in a position of power going into my negotiations; and that the General Manager wasn't particularly happy about that. He and I had butted heads on more than one occasion, and I wasn't someone he could put under his thumb with ease.

You have to understand that sometimes the **S.T.O.R.K.** comes with a power-trip and flies in holding many of the winning cards. When this happens, you need to take control of your own situation by doing what's best for you, as difficult as it might be. We were each other's **S.T.O.R.K.** It was no secret. And the GM was accustomed to always being the one in control with all the power.

Honestly, it shouldn't have been an issue. I loved doing the show. He should have loved my continued performance and the advertising revenue it was generating. It should have been a win-win situation for both of us, working synergistically for the benefit of each other and the company.

I didn't really want much, other than genuine talks about syndication for Gator and me, and our bonus structure being honored. That, and I really wanted decent coffee. I was already doing endorsements for the best coffee shop in town. I was going to ask for my own coffee blend to be delivered to the station, and then turn that into a revenue producer for both the company and the coffee shop. It was a silly thing to ask for, some might say a diva move, but I really couldn't think of much else I really wanted or needed.

That was until I came across a bit of information entirely by accident.

One of the on-air personalities made a flippant comment to me about how nice it must be to be paid as highly as I was, and knowing I was going to be getting more while he was going to have to find a part-time job somewhere. I was rather taken aback. I wasn't receiving an extreme salary as far as I knew. Plus, my salary wasn't a topic of discussion. At least it wasn't on my end. When I dismissed the comment, he kept on claiming he knew EXACTLY how much I was making. When I asked him how he supposedly knew, he walked me into a hallway between our on-air studio and the studio for the Hit Music station.

There, out for anyone walking by to see, was the paycheck for the other female morning show co-host.

My colleague pointed to it and said, "We all can do the math for how much per year that adds up to. And she isn't even CLOSE to having a #1-rated morning show, which means you're making a lot more than this."

I did do the math. Then I got angry. I wasn't making significantly more than she was. I was making significantly less. By about $10k. And that wasn't taking into account the bonuses she WAS being paid.

I was livid. I gave them every ounce of my talent and energy and built a successful show and station for them. But somehow there was no value in that? There was more value in the people who hadn't delivered than there was in me?

Once again, Howard's words rang out:

"When they try to screw you over (and they will), hold your ground and don't cave in. You know what's right and wrong, what's fair and what isn't. Make sure they know you know it too."

I was definitely going to make sure they knew it.

The day came for contract negotiations, and it started out with the normal niceties and small talk. Then the General Manager leaned in with his offer to stick with the current terms of our contract with a small bump for cost of living. He asked if that would work. I just calmly said, "no." When he asked what I wanted, I gave him a list of some silly things such as a company cell phone, a dry-cleaning allowance, and of course, my own coffee. We both laughed a bit and then he asked if there was anything else. This time I leaned in and said, "To be paid fairly and at least equally to the other morning show co-host's. Considering I generate more ratings and, consequently, more advertising revenue than all but one…and that one is my partner…I think it's about time you start giving me that professional respect and courtesy. The other items are negotiable. This is not." First, he turned white; then he turned red with irritation. He denied I wasn't being paid equally to every other morning show personality. Then he said I had no idea what anyone was being paid. So, I gave him the exact figure that was on the other female co-hosts paycheck, including taxes taken out and bonuses given. I didn't think a person could go that white. When I explained he ought to coach his favorite personalities on doing a better job of keeping their paychecks out of public sight, he went back to an angry red.

He said there was no way he could make that substantial of an increase in my salary. I didn't budge. When he asked how we were going to overcome this impasse, I explained that until they increased my salary, we couldn't and that I would be officially finished with my obligations to them. I didn't need to work. Chris made a comfortable amount. Or I could explore other options since, per the terms of my contract, if it was not renewed, my noncompete was null and void. You could have heard a pin drop. They knew I was right and could walk across the street without repercussion.

The meeting ended and I started preparing to clear my things out. We had a week. I meant it when I said I would walk.

Over the course of that week, they tried to offer me the little things from the list of silly items I had submitted, tried to offer bonuses that they already had not been delivering, and tried to make me feel guilty. It would hurt them, the listeners, and me because I loved the show. I wasn't swayed. I knew what was right, and I was holding firm.

The end of the week came, I packed up my things, and said my goodbyes wishing them well. I didn't get far before the General Manager reached out and asked if I could give him until the end of the month. He was working with corporate to try to move some things around. I agreed to an "at-will" contract through month's end. At the very end of the month, while it wasn't the exact figure I had asked for, I got a fair and equal salary, plus my coffee. Never again would I ever let anyone take advantage of me like they had again.

I also realized that this would be the beginning of the end. The GM would never allow me to have this much control over things. It was just a matter of time. The knives would come out. Time to keep my eyes and ears open.

It took less than a year before they started manufacturing accusations. Verbal warnings about being unpleasant in the hallways or using coarse language despite most of the men using cuss words as a greeting routinely. They went so far as to limit what I could say and how I could address colleagues in the building. I worked for a media company that was censoring my speech.

Then Hurricane Katrina hit, and Gator had lined up many people that were victims in the New Orleans area to speak freely on our show. It didn't paint the Governor in a positive light. We were trying to raise funds for relief and give people an honest report of what was happening in the area.

But after we did it, I got called on the carpet by management and blamed for creating conspiracies. My political affiliations were attacked for things I didn't say. Somehow it all rested on my shoulders. I took it because Gator would have done the same for me.

Les suddenly would no longer speak to me. He had banned me from the on-air studio when he was doing his midday shift and would not see me in his office. He wouldn't answer his phone. He simply cut me off completely. He would meet with Gator but would not allow me into the meetings and would not offer a reason. When Gator questioned him, he wouldn't give an answer. I was beside myself and frustrated. I had no idea what had happened, and it was hurtful. I adored Les. This was not like him at all.

It went on for weeks when Les finally asked if I'd meet him in the conference room after the show for a meeting. I happily agreed thinking I was going to finally hash things out with him and figure out what was going on. It was an ambush.

I was receiving a written warning for discriminatory practices against a coworker based on his sexual preferences. The kid who filled in with me when I kept bouncing between morning show partners. The same kid I gave money to so he could get the tires on his vehicle replaced without asking for a penny back. The kid I went out with frequently and socialized with regularly over the years. The same kid I had petitioned management to hire as my permanent morning show partner. The kid I looked at like he was my own kid brother. This was the person I was allegedly discriminating against. To this day I have no idea if he was in on this or not. The only thing I did know was that it was a setup.

On top of that, I was being written up for inflammatory remarks made against the GM and Les based upon hearsay. I could have maybe agreed with it to an extent if it had only been about the GM, but Les? Not a chance. I didn't always agree with Les, but I was loyal to him. It's why it was so difficult when he gave me the silent treatment.

When I asked for some sort of proof of these accusations… accusations I vehemently denied… and if I could at least have the courtesy of facing the people making the accusations, they refused. I wasn't allowed to know who filed the complaints, and there was no proof that I had said or done anything. It was based solely on "anonymous" reports, and it was my word against theirs. The problem was, my words didn't count, and I was facing disciplinary action for trumped up charges.

I finally looked at Les and told him I didn't care anymore what anyone else thought. The only opinion that mattered to me was his. I had decided if he believed in me, I would put up with whatever they were asking of me, but I had to know I still had his vote of confidence. I pleaded for him to at least have the decency to look at me and say something…anything. He gave a sideways look at the GM and never said a word. Not a single word.

The General Manager then ended the meeting by telling me I would be put on probation to determine if my behavior would improve, and I would receive a copy of the notes from the meeting. Did I understand what was expected of me going forward? Oh yes. I understood completely. They expected me to sign off on it and acknowledge what I had "done." I refused to do that. I hadn't done it, so I certainly wasn't going to sign off on it.

Les got up and rushed out at that point. He had left the building before I ever got out of the conference room. He had also turned off his cell phone.

All of this happened before noon on a Friday. The GM happily went to lunch, and I could hear people whispering in the hallway how management had finally stuck it to me and taught me who was boss. There was laughter and discussion about how much it would "suck" to be me, and there was nothing I could do about it because I was on probation.

Once again, Howard's words of wisdom rang loudly in my ears:

"At some point you will know when it's no longer worth the fight. When that day comes, leave on your terms; not theirs."

I found Gator and told him what was happening. It wasn't worth the fight any longer.

I had accomplished everything I had set out to do there. I was riding at the very top, and what an incredible ride it had been while it lasted. I knew there was no unfinished business left to handle.

At 2:30pm I called the General Manager and gave him my resignation effective immediately. He sounded genuinely shocked. They hadn't expected this. They thought they held all the cards. They thought wrong. He asked if I would reconsider and see how things turned out at the end of the probationary period. I explained that I could not work for a Program Director who no longer had confidence in me. It wasn't fair to him, to me, or to the listeners. I made arrangements to have Gator escort me through the building the following morning to pick up my things and leave my key and parking pass. I didn't want to cause any drama so I chose a day and time when I knew there would be the least amount of people there.

I took my things and left the radio complex, and my career in the radio industry, for the last time.

Then I went home, cried a bit to grieve the loss, felt almost a sense of relief…

…and I went out and ordered a slice of strawberry pie.

The greatest advice I can give you from this experience isn't even my own. I'll leave you with Howard's words. They were a gift given to me, and now I offer them to you when tackling life's hurdles:

1. *Trust your instinct and do what you do best. When they try to make you question yourself, double down and do it even harder.*

2. *They will try to take credit for what you do. Let them only up to a certain point. You know what you bring to the table. Make sure they do too.*

3. *Keep your head on a swivel and grow eyes in the back of your head. Keep your ears listening at all times. When the knives come out, at least you'll see it coming.*

4. *When they try to screw you over (and they will), hold your ground and don't cave in. You know what's right and wrong, what's fair and what isn't. Make sure they know you know it too.*

5. *At some point, you will know when it's no longer worth the fight. When that day comes, leave on your terms; not theirs.*

6. *Enjoy every minute of the ride while it lasts. When it's finished, make sure you have no regrets and no unfinished business.*

7. *Order the pie. Always order the pie.*

There are going to be times when you **C.R.O.A.K.** and all it does it get the attention of the **S.T.O.R.K.** You can try to **L.E.A.P.** but occasionally, that **S.T.O.R.K.** is just too big. The only way to prevent yourself from being swallowed alive is to walk away from the hurdle and find a new path to walk down. That's how a smart **F.R.O.G.** lives to succeed another day.

CHAPTER 11

HANGING UP THE HOLSTERS

It doesn't pay to get over the hurdles if you don't learn from them. Otherwise, you end up **L.E.A.P**.ing over the same hurdle over and over. That's not being a **F.R.O.G.** because you aren't **REFUSING** the **GARBAGE**. You're only transferring it to the next **S.T.O.R.K.** down the road. Despite what I thought, that's exactly what I was doing.

The next few months were a big reset. I would learn to sleep again (sort of). I would learn to be a wife and mother again (mostly). I would learn how to be Sheral again, instead of "Sher on the Air." It was odd to go out and have listeners ask me what happened and why I was gone. They were being told nothing. They felt abandoned. So did I. I did my best to tell them that I loved the show and them, but I couldn't stay any longer. It had become a toxic environment. I made sure they knew I was still loyal to Gator and encouraged them to stick with him. I found myself limiting where I would go. It felt like a forced breakup.

Gator left shortly after I did. The General Manager went after him too. It was all about control. The show immediately started dropping in the ratings. I felt badly about it, mostly for the listeners, but also for the gal they brought in as my replacement. She was the daughter of my morning show partner my first time around at the soft rock station. Extremely talented girl…just like her Daddy had been. I remember her coming to the station when she was just 9 years old. Howard would let her hang in the studio. She would have been amazing if she had been in the right environment, but she didn't have a chance at that place.

Even Les would be gone. Forced out just before he could retire and collect his pay. Gator had encouraged me to reach out and talk to him after the dust had settled. I'm glad I did. There were so many unanswered questions about why he had abandoned me. It turns out he was being pressured by the General Manager and Corporate to go after me. They were unhappy with how much they were paying me and how much "power" I had with my ratings. Imagine that…a radio company upset that I was delivering the exact thing they needed to stay in business and make revenue. They were threatening his retirement if he didn't somehow get me "under control." His hands were tied. He hated not being able to talk to me about what was happening and was upset about how things were handled. None of them had expected me to leave. They blamed him for allowing my departure and not convincing me to stay. They blamed him for the drop in ratings after I left. In the end it didn't matter what he had done, they let him go anyway. He never got his retirement pay, nor his benefits which included insurance. Les had been a **F.I.S.H.** in this situation and the **S.T.O.R.K.** had swallowed him alive. Had I known what they were doing to him, I likely would have stayed to protect him.

I was just happy to have finally gained an understanding of what had happened and found some closure. Our relationship was back to where it had been in the beginning. Sadly, it would be the last time we would speak to one another. Within a month Les suffered a massive stroke that left him unable to speak. He passed away in 2014 and is missed every day by those who knew him.

When we moved back to Kansas City in 2007, I knew I was done with commercial radio for good. Now it was a matter of figuring out who I was and what to do.

A few months after I left the radio station, we had the opportunity to transfer once again. We opted to head back to Kansas City for the familiarity. It was a great place to raise a family, big enough to enjoy great entertainment and restaurants, and Chris could return to the cockpit to fly.

I did my best to adapt to being a homemaker and mom, but as I said in an earlier chapter, it didn't come naturally to me. I loved my kids, but I'm not built to be the volunteer at the PTA or someone who joined book clubs and scrapping groups. I'm not crafty and I don't bake well! Everything is a skill, isn't it? I didn't have those skills. I was left feeling bored and incomplete, longing for something to fill the void. I'm a professional at heart. Likely a professional mess, but getting messy is what gets the job done, right? I just needed to find the right thing to get my hands dirty with once again.

I love to learn…especially when it involves people. If there's something that can give information to them, or if it's something that can bring people together, I'm all for learning it.

Connection with people. My passion/addiction is in the honest connection, that one-on-one interpersonal exchange with another human being. That in-the-moment bond that comes from the Power of a 5 Minute Conversation.

I found an unlikely candidate that would do all those things: wine.

No, I didn't become a wino! The days of drowning myself in a bottle are long-time done. What I discovered goes far beyond drinking it.

How do you learn the most about people? You look for things that tie to their culture, their geography, and their history. Look at their art, the food they eat, the work they do, and what brings them together.

Then take a look at wine from start to finish. It's a fantastic combination of agriculture, chemistry, artistry, history, geography, and culture all mixed up with a touch of Disney and Harry Potter magic. There is always something new to learn with each harvest, each presentation. It is a perfect connector, and teaches so much to both the beginner and the pro.

I fell in love with it immediately and learned everything I could. I travelled to various wine regions, talked to locals and producers alike, broke bread together over lively conversation and beautifully produced wine offerings, and completely immersed myself in the education. I became a Certified Specialist of Wine at the age of 40. I had no idea what I was going to do with that certification, but I had made the decision it was my path going forward. It was my singular passion and purpose.

When my Program Director Howard had said I would forever be a hired "gunslinger" until I found my own space, I always thought he meant within the radio industry. It turns out that "gunslinger" mentality applies everywhere across industries and in personal relationships.

I had the great fortune of being introduced to a wine broker/supplier through one of my best friends. They had gone to high school together and she thought he might be able to point me in the right direction to get me started within the wine and spirits industry. I reached out and we just clicked. Once again, the Power of a 5 Minute Conversation would come about. What I thought would be a quick chat ended up changing my life in ways I couldn't have dreamed of. I traveled with he and his Assistant Manager on a week-long whirlwind of a trip to Europe for the education of a lifetime. In return for video interviews of he, his associate, and their clients during business exchanges, I would meet winemakers, brokers, educators, and exporters from Spain and France. I would get a crash course from the inside on how the business worked, how to network, negotiate, and determine quality. It opened my eyes up (literally) to a world I had no idea existed. It changed me for the better. It gave me insight into views I hadn't considered, different ways of doing things, and challenged me to expand my horizons. There's always more than one way to see or accomplish something. It may not be the right way for you, but it will always give you a greater understanding and insight into others if you're aware of the options and ideas. It will allow you to create better connections, communications, and potential partnerships for success. I still strive to teach that idea to my children, my family, friends, and clients to maximize their odds of success as well.

Shortly after arriving back in the U.S., I would meet up with my new friend and mentor again for another life-changing introduction. A small wine distributor in St. Louis was looking to gain a foothold in Kansas City. They currently had someone working part-time who would make the drive from St. Louis once or twice a week, but they needed someone local who knew the area and could work to establish accounts on a full-time basis. I was pitched as being the right person to tackle that challenge. I met with the General Manager of the company. Seemed like a nice enough guy. We chatted, laughed, talked about my background and why I thought I could help him open the market despite having no experience in the wine and spirits industry. I told him my success would come down to two things: my ability to connect with people and my passion for the product. 4 months later I became the first full-time salesperson for the Kansas City market.

I went into an industry I knew virtually nothing about with no experience and no real training. My boss didn't expect me to do much. I didn't know I wasn't supposed to be able to succeed. I think that's one of the secrets to success. If you **REFUSE OTHER'S GARBAGE** of limiting beliefs and expectations, your chances for finding a way to make it work go up exponentially. In 6 months, I managed to establish a territory by myself and grew it to a size where my boss was forced to hire a couple more salespeople to handle the growth, and a driver to start delivering product weekly since it was too much to fit in the trunk of a car at this point.

The owner of the company and my boss seemed happily surprised. I thought things were looking up and inquired about being the regional manager for the team in KC. I was told we would discuss it.

The problem is, there never was any sort of discussion…about anything.

Instead, we would periodically get emails to tell us what was happening after the fact. My best accounts were taken away and given to the new sales guys. The guys were great and very experienced, but even they thought it was odd that there was no discussion about how to divide everything fairly. They admitted I was getting a raw deal. We would eventually work with each other and some disgruntled accounts to create a better balance between the three of us. The GM wasn't impressed.

Then came the inconsistencies in our deliveries and inventories. Our restaurant and retail store accounts were wondering when they could get products back in. We were wondering the same things. I'd call, text, and email but most often the inquiries were ignored. If I got an answer, it was a curt "We'll let you know an ETA when we have one" at best, a hostile "We will get it when we get it" at the worst. It wasn't unusual for the GM to lie to us and tell us it was the fault of our suppliers or that it was ordered, and on its way when it wasn't. We were often instructed to lie to our accounts and try to get them to substitute something else. Lying in business is something I couldn't do regardless of the situation. You can't build a solid rapport with anyone, professionally nor personally, if you don't have honesty and integrity. You are only as good as your word.

Looking for solutions, I went around the GM and reached out to the suppliers directly. I not only had a great rapport with my accounts, but with the representatives from each of the wine suppliers. They were equally frustrated, but we managed to get product to our accounts as frequently as possible. It wasn't costing the company anything outlandish nor causing financial setback. On the contrary, I had the product sold, as did my colleagues. But the problem wasn't about finances nor skills and ability. It was always about control…management's need for it, and my attempt to gain it when it was lacking. My good intentions were irrelevant. My reasoning didn't matter. It came down to a battle for control and it is a recipe for disaster in the business place when you don't have open communication and an agreed upon compromise or plan of action.

It becomes even more of an issue when you aren't aware…or don't care…that control is the heart of the problem. I don't know for certain if the GM was consciously aware of his need to win in our power struggle (though I think I could guess correctly), but personally I wasn't aware of my own need. All I could see was a problem that needed fixing to help the company and customer alike, one that could help myself and my colleagues, and I came up with solutions. Solutions that were creating problems on a different level. I had become a **H.O.P.P.E.R.** once again.

It's only recently that I have come to terms with the fact that I am a control freak, and even more recently that I've started addressing it so that it doesn't become a destructive trigger in my life. Now that I can recognize the signs of it in myself and in others, I can work through it. I didn't have any of that awareness while working for this company, however, and the GM wasn't looking for ways to coexist nor compromise in any way.

It wasn't long before he started making phone calls and surprise visits to my accounts in Kansas City to "make certain I was acting professionally." I don't know why he didn't think they'd tell me what he was doing. Like I said earlier, I had a great rapport with my accounts. He would repeatedly ask my colleagues if they thought I was putting in enough work and representing the company well. He'd ask them if they had the same frustrations as I had. Looking back, he had to have known they would tell me what he was doing. I'm not certain what he was hoping for. He loved the sales numbers I was putting up. I wasn't impressed and didn't hide my disgust.

The situation went from bad to worse the day I got robbed. I remember that day vividly. Tuesday morning just after 9am. I was filling up my vehicle at the gas station before making the rounds to visit accounts for the day. On the passenger side seat was the leather zip bag I used to hold invoices, checks I'd picked up, etc. While I was smart enough to always take the keys out of the ignition, it never occurred to me to lock my doors while I was standing next to the truck pumping gas. A guy walked up to me on my blind side and asked if I had spare cash so he could fill up his tank and get home. I told him I didn't (I really didn't) and put some distance between us. He was there with another guy. The other guy grabbed the bag. They took off in a white car. Police were called. Reports were filed. I was scared.

I called my boss to let him know what had happened. His response wasn't what I had expected. He thought I was lying to him. He thought I had either misplaced the bag or had stolen the checks. In fact, he was so convinced I was lying that he gave me a set of steps I had to complete by 5pm that day to PROVE myself:

1. I had to provide him with a file reference number for the police report, along with the name of the officers I spoke to and a phone number where he could reach them.

2. I needed to contact each account I had visited the past two business days, explain that my work bag was missing that had account checks in it, and ask if they had seen it. He would be following up to make certain I had contacted them.

3. I was to contact the accounts whose checks were in the bag and tell them personally that I had irresponsibly caused their checks to go missing and that they needed to cancel and reissue the checks. If any were charged a fee for stopping the checks, I would be responsible for it.

He also stated repeatedly that the gas station had cameras and he would be calling to check on the footage. I needed to understand that those cameras would show it if I was lying. I was physically sick to my stomach at this point. I hadn't just been violated once by thieves, but now a second time by the guy I worked for. I went home, cried, and got to work completing his "tasks" so I wouldn't be accused of something I hadn't done.

The only thing he ever said about it was, "I didn't think you would actually have a police report filed. The gas station's cameras didn't have a clear angle or clarity for the video. They said the police looked at it too. Just make sure you lock your doors from now on and get the new replacement checks from those accounts." No apology…nothing. In fact, an apology never would come. The most he would ever say was, "It sounded fishy, and I made a mistake." That was it.

Why didn't I leave after that? Because I was over 40 and brand new in a career field that I loved and wanted to stay in. My goal was to gain a bit more experience and transition into a position with a supplier. Most of the hires with other companies were either young people in their 20s or people with years of experience. I didn't fit either of those categories, so I mistakenly thought I needed to stay where I was and keep looking for a better opportunity.

The stress took its toll. I had already been diagnosed with Fibromyalgia, Chronic Fatigue Syndrome, and Celiac Disease. Now I was feeling worse. A trip to the doctor revealed the very beginnings of a breast cancer scare. I would start a program to knock it out, plus infusion therapy twice a week to mitigate any side effects, boost immunity, and keep up my energy. I asked to be put on part-time status so that I could focus on getting healthy but could still maintain accounts. I would be able to call, email, and text when I was in treatment or recovering at home but would still visit accounts in-person on the days when I was cleared to do so.

Instead of being concerned, compassionate, or anything else that you and I might consider to be appropriate, the first response by my GM was one of disbelief. Not shock that it was happening; he thought I was making it up. Once again, my integrity was being questioned in the worst possible way. At least he was consistent.

He asked for the doctor's name and where she was located. He also asked for a medical letter stating I needed time for treatment and rest due to my diagnosis. I got the letter and sent it to him, along with the name and number of my doctor. He'd have the info and know that once again, he was wrong.

He had the nerve to call my doctor and try to violate my HIPPA rights, trying to get details about diagnosis and my treatment plan.

I wouldn't have even known it had my doctor not called me to tell me what he was asking about. He even tried to make her believe he had permission from me to release that information. He didn't. She didn't give it to him.

There was no point in confronting him about it. It wouldn't make a difference to him.

I should have left and taken legal action against him and the company on my own, but I was told by more than a few colleagues and associates in the industry that if I did so, no one else would likely hire me. I would become too risky. The worst part? They were right. The laws are in place to protect employees but if you use them, you become damaged property within your industry. It's a not-so-secret secret. It's why most doctors won't testify against each other. It's no different anywhere else.

They agreed to let me work part-time. No more than 2 days a week. But he was also going to require me to give up most of my accounts to the other two sales reps. I wasn't going to be allowed to call, text, or do emails. I was being forced to give it up completely.

Before I go any further, I feel I need to point out that I don't feel like every man I've ever worked for or with is out to get me, or women in general. And not every male-dominated industry (like the two I had chosen) is a bad place for women either. I just didn't have very good luck. You will find bad people no matter the place or the industry. They will be awful regardless of sex, race, religion, or position in life.

But for every 1 bad person, you will find 10 that are decent and willing to do what they can to help you, respect you, and treat you fairly.

This was the case with my colleagues. Marc knew it was wrong. He used his position as the go-between/ KC contact to convince the GM that since we 3 KC salespeople knew the accounts and areas best, we should sit down and determine how best to divide them up. What the St. Louis office didn't know was that there would be no real change in account allocations. We would talk to each of my accounts to see if they were willing to continue working with me via phone and email until I was finished with my treatments, or if they would like one of the others to become their new sales representative. They all agreed to keep me. The St. Louis office couldn't convince them otherwise, so they begrudgingly accepted the working conditions. It was either that or lose the accounts. Money talks.

The animosity continued to grow and within a few months, the GM would decide to cut off all communication with me. From now on, anything I needed to discuss would go through my Kansas City colleague Marc. He would become the de facto regional manager. My calls, texts, and emails were literally being rejected. My female colleagues in St. Louis would reach out to me personally to tell me it wasn't just me he was targeting, but all the women within the company. His behavior was reported to the owner. It fell on deaf ears. When I inquired with the others about looking into legal action together for discriminatory practices and a hostile work environment, they shied away from it. No one wanted to deal with it. I decided to let it go. He was 4 hours away from me, so I rarely had to see him, and honestly, not having to talk to him at all was a relief in a lot of ways. Or at least I thought it would be. He began denying my requests for samples to take to show accounts and my deliveries were "accidentally" being shorted or missed altogether. He was doing his best to make my job impossible to accomplish.

It came to a head the day before Christmas. My family and I were going to be in California visiting my in-laws for the holiday. My husband and I had made plans to visit many of the wineries I had been privileged enough to work with and represent who were in Napa and Sonoma. I had made certain all the orders for the accounts were handled earlier in the week since Christmas and New Year's was the biggest and busiest wine time of the year for them. They needed to be certain they didn't run out of their top sellers.

We had been having problems for months with the deliveries being made on time and with the products being missed. I asked on more than one occasion if all the orders had been double checked and if there were any issues with deliveries. I was assured everything was fine. On the 23rd I had asked again if everything was good to go for the deliveries that were happening. It was being pushed to the last minute…delivered during the morning and afternoon of the 24th…Christmas Eve. I received a curt response back (via poor Marc as the go-between) that the delivery trucks were loaded at the loading docks, everything was accounted for, and there would be NO issues. Mid-morning on the 24th we received an email stating they couldn't get to the trucks because the docks were closed for the holiday, and no one was answering any phone calls. Nothing would arrive before the 26th. The notification didn't even come from the boss. It came from our delivery driver. You can imagine the flurry of email exchanges that took place asking what we were supposed to do. When the GM finally responded, his solution was to call our accounts and make up some sort of excuse.

I lost it. There was no way I was going to lie to my accounts, especially to protect him and the company. I had worked too hard to establish my reputation professionally. I emailed the GM and told him as much and asked him why he wasn't stepping up to contact them. It wasn't our mistake; it was his for not checking and telling us everything was handled when clearly it wasn't. His response back was "YOU WILL NOT SPEAK UNLESS YOU ARE SPOKEN TO!!! IS THAT UNDERSTOOD?!!?"

It most certainly was. I tendered my immediate resignation and then emailed all my accounts and supplier contacts. Without going into details, I explained that there had been an issue with deliveries and, as a result, I could no longer in good faith remain with the company. I directed them to contact the GM directly for inquiries regarding their shipments and thanked them for allowing me to work with each of them. I didn't even get an acknowledgement of my resignation from the GM. To this day he's never acknowledged it; to me at any rate.

You are only as good as your word. And my word was better than I thought.

3 months later I was working for another wine and spirits distributor/importer. I got the position thanks to the accounts and suppliers I had worked with at the other company. It was a terrific experience with an amazing manager and incredibly talented colleagues. I was fortunate to have had the opportunity to join them and looked forward to a long career. I would more than double the revenue in my territory my first year...most of which happened in the last 4 months...the time frame they kept telling me you can't make new sales

without being established. Someone might want to explain to these companies that's a myth!

The GM from the other company would eventually ask my former Kansas City colleagues how I was doing in my new position. They told him I was killing it. Surprisingly, he told them he figured I would be because I was exceptional at what I did. Then he asked them if they thought he maybe had over-reacted in handling the Christmas situation. They didn't hesitate to tell him he had, and that it was one of the dumbest things he could have done. Both of my colleagues moved on to other offers and left that company. The owner sold the company to a business owned and run by a woman. The GM was no longer employed there within a few months. I don't know if he left on his own or was fired. I don't really care. Karma happens.

What was the biggest takeaway from this experience? I learned that people who are insecure will do anything to prevent someone from succeeding if they think that someone might outshine or pose a threat to them. It comes down to confidence and control. They lack confidence in their own ability, so they feel forced to control the situations and people around them. It goes back to that **F.I.S.H./S.T.O.R.K.** combination I've been mentioning. When you become the desperate **F.I.S.H. IN SEARCH OF HELP**, but you can't find anyone to fix things the way you want, you lose your **RATIONAL KNOWLEDGE** and lash out while becoming the **S.T.O.R.K.**

I learned that I was still behaving as a **H.O.P.P.E.R.** (**H**oping **O**ur **P**roblems **P**romptly **E**xit **R**outinely). Remember, a **H.O.P.P.E.R.** doesn't care if someone else fixes the problem, or if they have to take matters into their own hands. I took it into my own hands and kept bouncing into that hurdle thinking somehow things would change and get better. I wasn't very good at changing that habit but would try to curb the behavior with the new company as best as I could.

What I hadn't learned was that being a "gunslinger" wasn't making my life better. It was leading me down the worst path possible.

Howard (my old Program Director) said I would forever be a hired "gunslinger" until I found my own space. I always thought he meant within the radio industry. It turns out that "gunslinger" mentality applies EVERYWHERE…across industries and in personal relationships.

But the problem with a "gunslinger" is they never really fit in. Pay attention and you'll see there's that one individual who sits on the sidelines or outside the "inner circles" until they're needed to fix, save, or improve a situation. That person might be you. You might be the one doing it to someone else. It makes the person in the position of "gunslinger" feel like an outsider. It makes them feel used or taken for granted. It isn't a fun feeling. Eventually, the "gunslinger" gets so used to being on the outside that they normalize it and stop paying attention to outside noises and voices. They only hear what they need to hear to get ahead and get the job done. They stop actively "listening" and miss important messages from others. They miss the things that matter. Often, they miss what is happening to the people they care about the most. That's exactly what happened to me. I almost learned it too late.

In the middle of my business success with the new company, that lesson would finally force me to learn it the hard way. My youngest attempted suicide on my birthday when she was 14. Thank God she didn't succeed. Thank God I was home that day.

That was the day I gave my notice at work and resigned my position as "gunslinger" permanently. Never again would I focus so hard on something that I stopped paying attention to the people that matter. It took a near-tragedy for me to learn the lesson. The hurdle wasn't getting ahead in a career. The hurdle was my relationship with working. I hadn't realized it was my way of escapism. It had become an unhealthy addiction. I had used the pursuit of a career to get away from the pain and abandonment I had felt in my childhood. I looked at it as the thing to make up for the time and experiences I had lost in my youth when I was injured. It was my "badge of honor" that I wore to say I didn't need to fit in...I was fine being a loner. I wasn't.

I used it to hide the fact I didn't know how to have a proper relationship with my spouse, my kids, my family, and my friends. It became the mask I wanted to wear to keep the world from seeing I was insecure, vulnerable, and scared. That hurdle nearly cost me my world.

When you sacrifice your family, your friends, and the people that matter for your career and become a workaholic, you become a **F.I.S.H.** and a **S.T.O.R.K.** at the same time. You're **IN SEARCH OF HELP**, or in this case, in search of external validation. You need others to notice your skills, your success, your importance. You chase that external validation to feel like you matter. But when you let it become an all-consuming addiction, it causes harm to you and to the people around you. It doesn't create happiness; it causes stress and pain. It turns you into the **S.T.O.R.K.** taking your rational knowledge…knowledge that you aren't being the person you need to be for the people who need you the most. You aren't the person you need to be for yourself. It will swallow you whole if you let it. It will destroy your whole life. It nearly took the life of my youngest and almost destroyed our lives as a result. Don't let it destroy yours.

CHAPTER 12

MY DAUGHTER'S VOICE

They say that those who don't learn from their mistakes are doomed to repeat them. I seemed to be a living example of that saying.

My career ambitions didn't teach me the greatest lesson that I should have learned. That lesson about what my purpose was…my true purpose.

I had spent so much time focusing on me and a need for having my own voice heard that I stopped listening to some of the most important voices. The quietest voices. The ones within my own home.

I was so caught up in "proving myself to everyone" that I stopped proving myself to my own family.

I wasn't being a very good mother, nor a very good wife.

When our youngest daughter Katy was born, I knew something wasn't right. It had been a stressful last couple of months of the pregnancy, and it wasn't just because of my career issues, Chris' military adventures, or our move back to Louisiana. She didn't laugh much or coo like other babies. She would get overstimulated and shriek uncontrollably if there was too much noise or activity around her. Even colors seemed to trigger her. She wouldn't sleep unless someone would hold her.

Doctors and family both insisted she was just a fussy baby. Friends thought I was being overprotective and coddling here. But a mom knows, even when she isn't particularly good at being a mom.

She didn't play and interact the same way our oldest daughter Devon had. While she seemed happy (when things were quiet and still) and didn't have any physical or health issues that were apparent, there was something I couldn't put a finger on. It felt like she was distant and not quite with us most of the time.

As she got older, we noticed her motor skills weren't great. She was clumsy and couldn't catch. She didn't make eye contact. She didn't talk much. Again, her pediatrician maintained that some kids just developed a little slower than others, but that everything seemed normal. We had nothing to be concerned about.

We tried to enroll her in youth soccer. She spent more time sitting in the middle of the field watching butterflies or rolling in the grass on the sidelines than she did paying attention to the game and attempting to play. The ball could bounce off her and she would be happily oblivious to what was going on. It didn't matter if it was soccer, swimming, or anything else. Whatever we signed her up for, it was always a similar situation.

She was happy, friendly, and smart. She observed everything and was incredibly funny. She loved animals. But there were still those things that nagged at me and didn't seem right.

She hated being outdoors and couldn't stand to feel grass or dirt on her skin.

She was terrified of insects.

She was terrified of kids in costume at Halloween…we couldn't even get near a Halloween store display. We couldn't even let her see a television commercial.

At one point she refused to go into swimming pools for over a year because she was deathly afraid sharks would eat her.

She was terrified of the bathtub because she was certain she would be sucked down the drain with the water. She also believed sharks could somehow show up there as well.

She was convinced the sun was going to explode.

I know it all sounds funny and the workings of an overactive imagination, but it wasn't funny to us. It was so bad we couldn't go places or do a lot of things. It was stressful to her and to us. Devon thought she was weird. So did some of the kids at school.

Katy tended to gravitate towards the younger kids. By the time she was in 3rd grade, most of her friends her own age had formed their own groups and left her behind. She was most comfortable talking about preschool cartoons and stories with the kids in kindergarten and 1st grade.

It was her "weirdness" and comfort with kids much younger than she was that started us down the path of losing her "voice" and her way.

She was 8 years old and in the 3rd grade heading to school on the bus. A boy a year older than her started bullying one of the kindergarten students…a girl all of 6 years old whom Katy had befriended. Katy intervened to get the boy and his friend to stop. They proceeded to gut-punch Katy until she threw up and the bus driver could stop it.

She went to the school, in tears, and reported it to her teacher and the principal.

We were never called about it. I didn't learn what had happened until Katy came home from school, visibly shaken and upset. She wouldn't speak for hours.

When I called the school, they refused to give names or discuss any details. They would not even allow Katy to sit down with the boys or learn their names. They tried to pass it off on the transportation department. When I called the transportation department, they also refused to give information and passed it back on to the school. The only thing done was the boy who instigated things was prevented from riding the bus for the duration of the week. That was it. It amounted to an inconvenience for his parents and didn't even register with the boy. But for Katy, it would be the start of a torment that nearly ended her life.

The people…the adults and authority figures she trusted to guide and protect her away from home…had failed her in every possible way. They betrayed her trust, and mine.

She was terrified to go to school. Terrified to ride the bus. Terrified of being around other kids. She stopped laughing and talking. She stopped enjoying anything.

Chris and I immediately found a counselor for her to help her emotionally and enrolled her in a local martial arts school for kids to help her build her confidence and at least give her a way to protect herself, God-forbid, if a situation like the bus ride ever occurred again.

Ironically, it was the martial art school that came to our rescue where the "bully boy" was concerned. About the 2nd week into her classes, Katy came home and was refusing to go back. The boy who had beaten her up on the bus was part of her class. I immediately took her back and asked her to identify him. When she did, I pulled the instructor aside and let him know. He was amazing. He brought both Katy and the boy into his office, explained that there was a code and way of conducting themselves if they were to be members of his school, and that the boy had broken every one of those rules. He asked Katy what she thought should be done. Being the kind heart that she is, she asked the instructor not to punish him. An apology would be acceptable to her. The instructor then asked the boy if he thought it was enough. To the boy's credit (and a credit to the instructor's teaching), he stated it wasn't enough. That a meeting needed to be done with his parents, and he needed to make up with it by extra laps in practice, and by kind deeds on the bus and to other students he had wronged. The martial arts school had done what the school should have done. It handled the situation respectfully and taught valuable lessons on accountability, responsibility, collaborative solutions, and that actions have consequences. It had restored some of the trust Katy had in adults and figures of authority, and all seemed to go well for a time.

Counseling didn't go as well. Katy would not fully open up, despite liking her counselor. Even after years of building a relationship, she found it difficult to share what she was feeling and nearly impossible to put it into words. Katy's voice was invisible.

As she approached her teenage years, her motor skills continued to fall behind that of her peers. She hated writing because it was difficult to hold a pen or pencil without it hurting. It was difficult enough for her to vocalize her thoughts, let alone write them into a structured format.

She continued to cling to interests that were typical of kids much younger than she was. She couldn't relate to her peers, nor they to her. Finding friends was nearly impossible. Her counselor suspected that it was more than just emotional distress caused by the bullying incident. The counselor believed she was Autistic. This came around the time she turned 12. She would find a psychiatrist to facilitate testing if we wanted it. Our biggest concern was finding someone who would do the testing only and not insist on putting her on a bunch of different medications. She was already on a low-grade medication for ADD to help her maintain her focus. I hated it because she seemed like she was in a coma, but she begged to stay on it because it was the only time she felt like she could stay checked-in on what was happening around her without being overwhelmed. We chose not to get her tested because we feared it would make her feel different and not capable. In hindsight, this might have been the greatest mistake I ever made.

Middle school came and she seemed to thrive in her classes. She was still struggling socially and wasn't caught up emotionally with her peers, but she was happy. She was incredibly happy with her teachers, and so was I. We had a strong relationship built and were on the same page. I was hopeful we could find a way to get her more involved in groups where she would develop friendships and start relating to her peers before entering high school. I was very worried about how she would handle the break from teachers she trusted, and a school of 800 students instead of a couple hundred in middle school. But I was confident we'd make the transition successful. I needed it to be.

I was already overwhelmed with building a sales territory for work and battling her older sister. Devon and I had been like oil and water for years, and it only seemed to get worse as she got older. Chris and I were struggling to make our second marriage work with the stress of all of it. I didn't have it in me to tackle another crisis within the family. I had been dealing with enough of life's hurdles being thrown at me.

But then came the series of unfortunate events.

Devon (who wasn't just Katy's sister but also her best friend at the time) graduated from college and moved out of state. Katy was crushed.

Her cat was killed in an unexpected accident. He was who she considered her very best friend.

Our dog died.

Katy no longer got invited to birthday parties nor sleepovers. She sat alone in the cafeteria at school.

Her counselor left her private practice and moved away. She refused to see someone new.

Then came high school. It's scary enough for a 14-year-old starting her freshman year. It's a nightmare for someone who was struggling with her issues.

She had no friends.

I watched her grow sullen and more distant each day. I was helpless and couldn't reach her.

I pushed to get her into a few social groups, trying to get her some friends. She wasn't interested.

Then she started pulling out her hair. They call it trichotillomania- a compulsive disorder with an uncontrollable urge to pull out one's hair during times of stress. She had nearly pulled the hair under the back of her top layer of hair down to the bare scalp. For 3 years she had no eyebrows or eyelashes. She didn't want to be seen in public. Pictures were tortuous. She was told she looked like an alien from outer space.

In January of 2018, at the age of 14, on the weekend of my birthday, she attempted suicide. She had taken some pills and cut herself. Once she had done it, she got very scared and came to me. Thank God I was home. Thank God she had come out of her room.

I rushed her to Children's Mercy Hospital where they evaluated her. She was calm then. Tired and embarrassed but almost relieved we knew the anguish she was feeling. That anguish wasn't going to be done for a while.

Fortunately, she hadn't cut herself too deeply, and she hadn't taken enough of anything to warrant a stomach pump. Physically she was okay. Mentally she was not.

The hospital convinced us that it would be best to take her to a treatment center for evaluation. They told us they could connect us with psychiatrists and counselors who would be able to help us and get her set up with therapy. They could do an overnight observation and get things set up for us. We trusted them and agreed. Once they got our signatures everything changed.

They took her by ambulance and wouldn't allow us to ride with her.

Once we arrived at the facility, a run-down, dismal place filled with screaming adults and children alike, broken doors, and hopeless faces, we knew this was NOT the place for Katy to get help.

What we didn't know is once she arrived, we had NO rights as parents. They kept her at a psychiatric hospital against her will and ours. What we were told would be an overnight monitoring situation turned into a week of fighting and pleading to let her come home. She would cry and beg me to "Please bring me home. I promise I'll be good. I promise I'll change. Please, Mom…please bring me home." I can't tell you the amount of heartbreak I felt and tears that I've cried…that I still feel and cry to this day when I think about it.

We were limited to 45-minute visits and 10-minute phone calls. This was the second time an "institution" had let us down. But what was worse was that I knew I had let her down. I had let both of my children down by not being present enough. I couldn't understand what they wanted or needed. I couldn't hear them. They had an "invisible voice." It caused one to shut me out and move away. It almost took the other away from me permanently.

I should have known better and done more. I had grown up in a situation where I would have had an invisible voice had it not been for my mother. I should have done the same for my own children.

After a week of pure hell and mental/emotional torture for all of us, she was finally released. I had quit my job and committed to rebuilding our family. I was dedicated to making sure her voice would grow strong and always be heard.

We would never depend on another person or organization again where her well-being was concerned. And my recommendation is you shouldn't either. If you are a parent, you need to use the people and groups as a tool to facilitate, but not as your one and only solution. They don't have your family's full and best interests at heart. YOU do. YOU need to be the one to step up. I had to learn this the hard way. My daughter NEEDED me to become both an advocate, and a "rottweiler mom" to protect her and make certain her best interests and needs were being met. It wasn't going to win me any awards as a beloved parent with her school, nor her doctors. I didn't care. She was my daughter and that should mean something. It meant everything to me. It should mean the same to you. I hope it does.

The next 3 years wouldn't be easy for either of us. But we overcame the **S.T.O.R.K.S** and managed to **L.E.A.P.** the hurdles together.

Katy transitioned back into a normal classroom setting and brought failing grades up to A's and B's. We agreed as a family to get an official Autism/Asperger's diagnosis to make her eligible to receive accommodations for testing and classroom settings. She was relieved to know there was a reason for her struggles in the classroom and socially. She could finally focus on steps to work around it.

She got involved in two social clubs at the school and began to develop stronger socialization skills. She built a solid core of friends that get together frequently, even now that they've all graduated. Katy is now considered the social "ringleader" of the bunch.

During the Covid lockdowns, virtual learning was a nightmare with no proper guidance and ridiculous inconsistencies from the school district. Teachers were left to figure things out on their own. Some were amazing. Others didn't do much in the way of teaching. Katy was in a panic due to confusion and assignments being missed. Her grades began to slip again. I took the reins and taught her myself. Weekly battles with her school and the school board were heated. I'm certain they were happy to see me go when Katy graduated in 2021. To be honest, I was glad to be gone and have her out as well. Instead of working more closely with her during her virtual sessions and once classes were in-person, they often gave her a simplified version of her homework or omitted it completely. They told me she couldn't handle it. I argued she was plenty smart enough (I had seen what she could do and learn myself during lockdowns), but they weren't working with her the way they said they would within her IEP (Individualized Education Plan). She was supposed to have time one-on-one with one of their professionals to work with her. She didn't learn the same as everyone else. They failed to deliver.

This same school told me we should reach out to get an adult advisor to help Katy find help with housing and employment because she likely couldn't handle it herself going forward. They also told us she would never get into college because she didn't score well on her ACT tests. They didn't mention the Accuplacer alternatives you could take for community colleges. They suggested sending her to a program that made her "feel" like she was getting the college experience. The one that suggested it? Her Occupational Therapist at the school. I had all I could do to restrain myself across the table from her when she made that comment.

I'm happy to state that Katy is enjoying her first semester of community college currently. Real college. Not some program to give her the feeling she is participating. The college has offered accommodations for test taking because she isn't a great standardized test taker. So far, she hasn't needed the accommodations. She loves her classes and the change in the approach to learning. She is getting all As and Bs without help. Once she completes her 2 years, we will look at whether to finish at a 4-year college or move on to a specific program offered in her field of study.

What has she decided to get her degree in?

Communications, because as she told me, she "learned how to use her voice and make it strong." Her theater instructor said her voice was powerful. She told me she found it by listening to what I had told her and following my example. She gave me my purpose without even realizing it. That is the greatest testimonial I will ever receive. I will always be grateful to her for that gift. I couldn't be prouder of the woman she is becoming.

Going through this experience with Katy changed many things for the better. I don't have to worry if she is going to make it on her own anymore. She will. She's happy and determined. She's growing up.

She is driving and has a full set of eyebrows and eyelashes again! She's beautiful, both inside and out.

I learned to be more patient and persistent. I even fixed my relationship with my oldest daughter Devon again. She was my original "happiness." She still is. I couldn't be more fortunate. She is an exceptionally talented artist and an exceptional human being.

Our story here was fortunate enough to receive something many families don't get in situations like this: a happy ending.

It's nearly impossible to bounce back from a hurdle like this. You will feel guilt, feelings of failure, and total inadequacy. There will be fear. There is desperation.

I hadn't been a **F.R.O.G.** when it came to my family. I was both a **F.I.S.H.** and a **S.T.O.R.K.** I had nearly swallowed us all whole. I hadn't learned to **L.E.A.P.** any hurdles…and I certainly hadn't taught my children how to be resilient enough to get over them. Thankfully we had the chance to change things over time. Fortunately, our story has a happy ending. For many families, it's a tragedy.

If you're trying to navigate the waters with your children, especially those with special needs, please don't give up on them or on yourself. You are NOT alone. There are people and places to support you. If you don't know where to find them, reach out to friends, family. Heck, you can reach out to me. I will provide my contact information at the end of the book and try to connect you to people and resources that WILL help without trying to take over. Remember, YOU are your best advocate for your kids, and for YOURSELF. Do NOT forget to take care of YOU during this time. You're only strong enough to help others when you keep yourself strong too.

CHAPTER 13

HOW THE S.T.O.R.K. NEARLY DID ME IN

There's a saying that states "practice what you preach." That's not always easy to do, is it? It's easy to give others advice but how often do we follow it ourselves?

I just finished telling you in the last chapter that you have to remember to take care of yourself. True confession: I wasn't. I hadn't been for years.

I had promised myself I'd never stop paying attention to the people that mattered after the incident with my daughter. I broke that promise. I stopped paying attention to myself. Maybe I didn't break that promise after all, because honestly, I didn't think I mattered. At least not as much as everyone around me.

I had invested all my energy into my family and friends that I had completely forgotten who I was. I had shut the door on me and my needs to focus on everyone else. When people asked me what I liked, I couldn't tell them. I had no clue what I got excited about or took joy in anymore. It was like self-induced amnesia. I felt numb on the good days, hopelessly miserable on the bad days. But every day I did my best to convince myself and everyone around me that I was happy. Walking the dogs, planning nightly dinner, checking on homework situations, and playing personal assistant whenever I was needed. Friends said they wished they had my easy life. I wished I could trade with them. I don't know how homemakers do it without losing their minds. There is NOTHING easy about it. You work 24/7 and are often overlooked and taken for granted. It's the same tasks on a never-ending loop. Wash, rinse, repeat…every single day. Stay-at-home moms and dads are horrifically underappreciated.

Somewhere during this time, I started kayaking. I can't even remember when or how it came about. One day I just bought a cheap, plastic kayak and started paddling around our local lake. Then I was planning summer vacations with the family to do extended float trips in the Ozarks. Chris mentioned some crazy 340-mile race along the Missouri River that took place each year and suddenly I had a racing kayak and a coach. It turned out to be one of the best things that ever happened to me. It was something I could do for long periods of time without my health issues or my age interfering. It gave back as much as I was willing to put into it. I finally had something to be passionate about again. It reminded me I still had some fire and drive. It was the start of finding my way back to me.

The other thing I did right was reconnect with some friends I grew up with and hadn't seen since high school. I wasn't close friends with them growing up, in fact, a couple of us hadn't even been friends at all. It's amazing how when you get fully into adulthood, you discover that your greatest support comes from the unlikeliest of places. These 3 ladies are amazing in their desire to support, inspire, and band together with unbreakable loyalty. We talk daily even if it's just to check in. They were a much-needed gift to me.

One of the gals in this group of unlikely sisters was instrumental for getting me back on my feet and pushed me in ways I had never considered. Julie Traxler came from an extensive corporate background and had recently launched a business of her own, SB PACE, to help small businesses. She is fiercely driven, always educating herself, and sometimes a little direct. I admired what she was doing, even if I thought she was a bit of a crazy workaholic.

What I had never realized was how smart she was. Like I said, we weren't friends growing up. We sort of connected by accident a few years ago, but it developed into a strong connection and friendship.

The one thing I don't think she could quite figure out initially was why I wasn't doing anything professionally. If I'm going to be honest, it was because I didn't think I was capable nor desirable in the work force any longer. I had been out for a few years focusing solely on Katy. My skill set was unique, and I wasn't certain how it fit into other industries. I didn't want to go back to radio, and I didn't want to go back to schlepping products 8-12 hours a day for a wine and spirits distributor. Plus, I was hovering in the "middle aged" gray area where businesses start overlooking women. Or at least that's what I thought and had been told. I didn't know what I wanted to do, where to look, or if I'd even enjoy any position I took. I was AFRAID of disappointment. I had created a **S.T.O.R.K.** for myself and was letting it swallow me alive.

Julie wasn't the type to let skill go to waste though. There was a day she came to our group chat and asked us to read through an ad she had written and give feedback. I got to it first and asked if I could tweak it a bit and send it back to her. She agreed and 30-minutes later I gave her copy she wanted to use. I was excited to be able to help her but didn't think much about it. She came back again with another script for copy. Once again, I rewrote it and gave it back to her. She liked it and used it.

The next day she emailed me and asked me if I thought I could write copy without reworking it. She gave me the details and the audience she was looking to connect to. Once again, I wrote it and sent a full copy ad back to her. This was followed by a reply telling me I was a copywriter and to be prepared for a Zoom meeting later that week...I would be meeting the team and my new client.

Client? Client for what? It turns out she had a new client that she was helping to launch a new business. They needed someone who could write the copy for the entire website prior to product launch and handle the email campaign. That person was me. I suddenly found myself back in the professional world.

It was amazing being part of her team. Julie introduced me to others within the team and I began an amazing journey of rediscovering my skills, my potential, and my love of working with people. Turns out I was capable after all. I had been a **F.I.S.H. IN SEARCH OF HELP** and hadn't even realized it.

It didn't stop there though.

At the end of a successful project with her client, I made the decision to launch my own copywriting business. I had always toyed with the idea of owning a business, but I never could figure out what to do and I had no clue how to start.

Julie and her partner handled everything from start to finish. She helped me turn what had always been a fleeting dream in the background into a reality.

We collaborated on several projects together over the next few months. I continued to learn new things about copywriting and business in general.

And then she introduced me to a whole new world.

One of the people she introduced me to was a guy by the name of Tony Whatley. Tony is an insanely successful entrepreneur who mentors and coaches other entrepreneurs. Julie had connected with him and was going to an event he hosted. It was a combination mastermind and vacation for like-minded entrepreneurs who could network, exchange ideas, develop lasting partnerships and friendships, and learn from some of the top experts in various industries. It sounded amazing! I joined his 365 Driven Society and purchased my spot to his ADVANCE. I headed to Montana with great anticipation hoping for fresh perspective, great tips, and some much needed motivation.

Let me repeat that… I was looking for motivation…because I didn't have any.

Within months of starting my business, my gut told me I had made a mistake. Everything in me was telling me copywriting wasn't what I was supposed to be doing, but I didn't want to switch directions. I was listening to those who had more experience than I had saying that to find success and joy in your business, you had to give it time and stop chasing every new idea that came along. I felt like I had to stick with it and figure out how to make it work. I didn't want anyone to think I was a flake. I didn't want to disappoint family and friends who had supported and invested their time in me. The problem was, I was disappointing myself. The only thing I had become good at was keeping that **F.I.S.H.** mentality and looking for someone else to help me get on track. I had created yet another **S.T.O.R.K.** for myself in the process.

Remember how I've said **S.T.O.R.K.**s **TAKE** all **RATIONAL KNOWLEDGE** from you? I got hit by a whole flock of them at that event. And they were all invited in by me. It was as if I had opened the door wide and presented them with a formal invitation to come on in.

I was at this beautiful resort surrounded by unimaginable beauty and 40+ dynamic entrepreneurs. I was learning from some of the most exceptional human beings I had ever encountered who willingly shared their knowledge, their time and energy, and their friendship with me. We laughed, learned, and played together for hours. I made connections and built relationships that will last a lifetime.

And yet I didn't feel like I belonged there. I didn't think I deserved to be there. I felt like a fraud.

You might be thinking I had what is known as "imposter syndrome."

Let's take a second to discuss Imposter Syndrome. It's a lie...a myth. You aren't dressing up as a police officer and arresting people (at least I hope not since that's totally illegal). Pretending to be something you aren't and trying to make someone believe it makes you an imposter. In some cases, you're looking for someone to do your job for you so you can take credit for doing it. In that case, you're also an imposter. But if you are in a business as an accountant, a mechanic, or in my case, a copywriter, you aren't pretending to be those things. You ARE those things. What you're doing isn't Imposter Syndrome; you aren't looking to prove you are what you say you are. You're looking for either external validation that you're good at what you're doing, or you're looking for someone to tell you how to do it better. That doesn't make you an imposter. That makes you a **F.I.S.H.**

That wasn't my issue. I knew what I was. I was fully capable and provided good work. I even knew what I needed to do to build it up over time.

I just didn't like it. In fact, I had come to loathe it. I felt like a miserable employee trapped within my own business. I would wake up and dread knowing I had to work on any of it.

A huge problem for me came from feeling like I would be looked at as a failure if I stopped copywriting. Or I'd be seen as one of those people that jumps from idea to idea without ever sticking with anything. Someone who doesn't wait long enough for it to grow and become successful. They quit too soon. I didn't want to be a quitter. I didn't want to look like a flake.

I'm not sure how many people at that event even knew I did copywriting. Mostly because I didn't tell anyone. I spent more time talking about my upcoming kayak races and my former professions in radio and the wine and spirits industries than I did about my current business. I'm certain they were confused about who I was and what my actual purpose was because I was just as confused. I had a business, but no purpose and no passion.

Listening to those brilliant speakers and entrepreneurs, hearing and seeing the excitement they had for what they were doing and how they were helping others amplified that little voice inside me telling me, "You've made a mistake." I was worried that everyone there would look at me and know it.

I was too insecure to do what was best for me and was letting fear run my life. Fear of things that weren't even real. Fear of things that didn't matter.

But my biggest fear was that someone would ask me what I wanted to do if I didn't want to be a copywriter. What did I want to do instead? I didn't have an answer for that question, at least not one with any clarity that would allow me to revamp the business and move forward. I honestly didn't know what I wanted to do. I created my own invisible voice out of FEAR.

It wasn't all fear and self-loathing for me though. Despite myself, I gained HUGE amounts of knowledge and tools I could use to improve myself both personally and professionally. That's how incredible these events are. I got value even while I was in the middle of self-sabotage. And the people I connected with while I was there? That might be the greatest part of it all!

One of those people that I met on the first night was a woman named Lauren Johnson.

I had no idea who this beautiful, young woman was when she appeared next to me out of nowhere. It was as though she just materialized out of thin air, but her presence was powerful when she arrived.

I don't believe in chance meetings. I genuinely believe that everyone you meet is there for a reason. They are either there to give you a gift, or you give one to them. It's just a matter of whether you're paying attention and looking for it. Some gifts are good, some bad. Sometimes it's something simple that gives you a laugh or a smile in passing to brighten your day. Other times it's powerful enough to change, or even save, your life. I knew meeting her was significant. I hadn't figured out why though.

We chatted about the upcoming kayak races I was training for. It turns out Lauren was a Mental Performance Coach. She had worked for the New York Yankees organization helping the athletes work through their obstacles and had now set up her own coaching business. I thought maybe she was in my life now to help me power through the tough spots I might encounter during my races. She talked to me about owning my "3-foot space" and learning to control the little things around me when everything else seemed out of my control. I remember her telling me it's a lot like climbing the side of a mountain. If you look up to see how far you have left to climb, it becomes overwhelming. If you look down to see how far up you are, fear comes in and you risk either becoming paralyzed or you fall. If you focus on your 3-foot space, you are only looking for the next space to step into or hold on to. Each small step moves you out of your "discomfort zone" and gets you further to accomplishing your goal and reaching the top. It was incredible advice and I thought it would come in handy.

It would come into play, but not for my races and not in any way I had imagined.

Three days after that conversation, and the final day of our event, we went hiking in Glacier National Park. Against my better judgment, I went with the more advanced group to push myself past my comfort zone. This "old-ish", chunky gal huffed and puffed trying her best to keep up and make it to the top. 3-foot space advice and TREMENDOUS support from those around me got me to the top. I couldn't have been more excited. I did something that no one, including myself, thought I could do. I didn't quit. I made it.

I thought getting to the top was the tough part. Going down was what caught me by surprise.

Remember that ankle injury and the wrong leg operation I talked about way back in Chapter 4? Yeah, that one. It came back. 30+ years of being physically strong and overcoming that hurdle, and it showed up again without warning.

We were on the last half mile after successfully hiking the mountain. We weren't even in a rough area or on any sort of decline/incline. It was a flat, even path. I was laughing with my friends, excited that I had done it and that they had been there to support me.

That's when I heard and felt the "pop" in the right ankle.

I didn't twist it or trip. It simply gave out. What I hadn't known is that the surgery they had done on me had a shelf-life. It was a matter of time before this was going to happen and I was long past the time they expected it to last. I just didn't know it.

Special thanks to my "family" in this photo. I owe you one:

My friends helped me get to the shuttle bus. I could hear the whispers from some of the others that I never should have attempted the hike. That I had no business doing it. I didn't have the experience. I was out of shape. The usual negative comments. I will tell you now that I have NO regrets and I absolutely SHOULD have done it. I'm GLAD I did it. That's what entrepreneurs do. We push past our comfort zones striving to be better. Sometimes we take a hit along the way. Then we help each other move forward until we can stand and do it on our own. I made it with support. I know what I can accomplish now. And I know that when I'm down, I have people I can count on to help me back up. I will do the same for them anytime now. That's a promise for life.

But I didn't have that mindset and clarity then. I was broken. Mentally, physically, and emotionally. I had never truly worked through the trauma of the original injury. I just simply closed the door on it because I never thought it would come back. Now I was faced with crutches and wheelchairs again. I wasn't as physically capable as I was in my teens.

My racing season was gone and so was my confidence. I was embarrassed. I was angry. I was sad. At that moment, I crawled headfirst into the mouth of the biggest **S.T.O.R.K.** I could create and mentally begged it to swallow me whole. I don't even recognize the person I was then. That person who kept looking back at me in the mirror, that person had embraced being a victim, a quitter, and a failure. It's horrible and embarrassing for me to think back on it. I know that I lost the respect of some of the people I met at that event because of it. I had lost respect for myself too. But I also can give myself a bit of grace now and understand it's part of being human. We never know what the trigger will be that breaks us. What seems trivial or ridiculous to one person could be the one thing…that one piece of baggage and trauma…that we have never figured out how to work through that overwhelms us and stops us in our tracks. My experience has changed the way I look at people going through their own crisis. I might not understand, but now I look to see if there is a way I can throw them a lifeline and pull them out of that deep hole.

Each person has that one hurdle they have turned into a mountain. In my case, it really WAS a mountain. Well, at least there was a mountain involved, but the real issue was my inability to handle loss of control and loss of my identity. Loss in general. From childhood on, I never learned how to handle having things taken away and having no control of it. It's why I clung so tightly to racing. It was my symbol of who I was, something that was purely mine and brought me joy. Now it was gone, and I couldn't see past the hurdle.

For 4 months I let myself self-destruct. My business was all but gone because I couldn't bring myself to write content for clients or post on social media. When I tried, it was awful and without focus. I wasn't marketing. I wasn't working. I wasn't doing anything but drowning in a pool of my own pity. It was gross.

Lauren jumped in and began coaching me to build up that mental toughness. We started creating and implementing plans to rebuild everything and figure out what was standing in the way of making the mental and emotional **L.E.A.P.** out of the hole I had dug for myself. I learned what the 3-foot space meant- just focus on what you can control in the 3-foot space surrounding you.

It started with the first step of forcing myself to show my face professionally and focus on the things I could do: content creation, writing, and speaking.

It didn't matter how bad it was, it just mattered that I was taking the steps and working to move forward using the tools I still could control.

I began working with a physical therapist. There was no way to fix the injuries (the other ankle would give way shortly after the mountain incident). But there were ways to strengthen the muscles around it to ease the workload. There were ways to improve the structure to create more strength and flexibility. We were creating "work-arounds" so that I could go back to the life I enjoyed physically.

I kept working with Julie who was hellbent on getting me back into the saddle of creative writing. She stayed on me, giving me projects that I shouldn't have been attempting in the state of mind I was in.

I didn't miss a meeting with Lauren, nor any of the "homework" assignments to dig deeper and discover what was really at the source of my problems.

And it worked. By September I was building a business presence back up and my copywriting was back to being on point. With a lot of help, I managed to get back in the kayak and on the water. No racing, but it was a start. Everything was starting to come back.

That's the biggest lesson you can learn from this experience. It doesn't matter how far you fall. It doesn't matter what you've lost, or THINK you've lost. You can build it back up. You just have to take that first step, or first crawl to pull yourself up by inches. It doesn't matter what anyone else thinks of you. They're going to judge you on your way back up. Let them. Use it as fuel to prove them wrong. Just don't give up on yourself. Be the **F.R.O.G.** and never give up. Don't be afraid to let others hold you up while you're scratching and clawing for that next foot hold. **REFUSE OTHER'S GARBAGE**, even if that garbage is your own. You are capable, even if you can't see it or don't know it. I know it. I believe in you. Just take the step.

CHAPTER 14

THE POWER OF A 5-MINUTE CONVERSATION

I wish I could tell you that I took my own advice that I left you with in the last chapter. I didn't; at least not at first. It seems I have had to learn the most important lessons the hard way.

Like I said, I was slowly getting my life back on track. I was putting myself back together physically, and mentally focusing on giving my business the attention I thought it deserved. Both still felt like a chore, but I was convinced I just hadn't been giving enough to either task. No matter what you're doing, there are going to be times where you don't like it, but you have to do those things if you intend to succeed. There will be those times where you have to "embrace the suck" in everything from personal relationships to business. I just chalked this up to being part of the "suck."

It was during this time that I decided to go to my second 365 Driven Advance. I didn't feel like I asked enough questions or took advantage of the knowledge and networking opportunities at the first one. And I had a chip on my shoulder after the dreaded ankle incident. I wanted to prove to myself that I belonged in every way possible.

This time it would be held in Tucson, Arizona, and the speakers that would be there had really piqued my interest. Media focus, professional speaking, magazines, podcasting, SEO, and marketing…all the things that got me fired up and excited. All things I felt would help me tremendously within my business. I was looking forward to it.

I carried that enthusiasm with me on a visit to see my mom for a long weekend at her home in the Black Hills of South Dakota. Normally I visited her every year during the Sturgis Biker Rally. We would go for long rides, attend concerts together (yes, I took my mom to see Ozzy Osbourne, Kid Rock, and Fozzy amongst others…she loved it!), and have all sorts of crazy adventures. This year she wanted to skip it, so I chose to come up for a belated birthday and keep things a little more low-key.

It was a good visit, but I could tell something wasn't right. She didn't look well. She didn't act the same way she usually did. She wanted to make certain we did a few of the things we had talked about doing before I left. We went to the Buffalo Roundup in Custer State Park and watched them corral over 1200 head of bison to count and tag before releasing them back into the park for the winter. It was amazing.

We took a "Girls' Adventure Day" into Rapid City the day before I left to head home. It was a magical day filled with laughs and exploration. We talked candidly about anything and everything. One of the conversations that came up was about health and happiness. Mom had a way of dodging questions about herself and would almost always successfully turn it around so she could ask questions about the other person. When I had asked one too many questions about doctors and testing, she flipped it on me.

Mom asked me how things were going with the business. I told her everything was back on track after a shaky start. I just needed to focus and rework my plan of attack. She said, "Are you sure, because I've never known you to struggle with anything unless your heart wasn't in it. It's almost as if you're clinging to it because you THINK it's what you're supposed to be doing instead of it being something you love to do. What is it you're afraid of?" Mom was smart and always observant.

But being my mother's child, I was good at deflecting as well. I couldn't admit to her I was afraid of anything because that would mean I'd have to admit it to myself. So instead, I told her I was fine, just tired, but things were getting better. And I thought they were. I just needed to keep going.

Had I been honest with her (and to myself) I would have admitted that I was afraid I had made a mistake with my choice of business. I found it interesting, but I wasn't passionate about it. I had invested so much in the way of finances, time, and energy that I couldn't admit I might have been wrong.

I couldn't admit that I was second-guessing myself daily and having feelings of guilt continuously. Was I not giving it enough of a chance? Did I just need to give it more time? Was I not focused on the right things, the right education and courses, did I need to niche down?

I was afraid to tell her and admit to myself that I had no clue what I wanted to do anymore. I had zero confidence in myself and my abilities. The only thing I knew was I wasn't a quitter. So, I just kept headbutting the hurdle, hoping it would eventually give way so I could move forward. The only thing I was accomplishing was beating myself up…and I was afraid to admit that too.

When I got ready to leave the next day, I stopped in to say goodbye to the family. Mom was in bed, running a fever. She didn't look good at all. I wanted to stay and take care of her, but she insisted I needed to go. She was just run-down with allergies and had overdone it. Reluctantly I kissed her on the forehead and told her goodbye. While I drove away something told me that would be the last time I would ever see her.

Three hours into my drive she was admitted into the hospital. They would release her 3 weeks later to go home but wanted her to come back for a series of tests. They weren't entirely sure what was wrong, or at least that's what she had told all of us.

On October 25th my brother messaged me with great concern. He wanted to call an ambulance because Mom wasn't sounding right and looked gray. She was refusing to go into the ER. I called her and argued with her. She sounded like she was having trouble breathing. We argued for about 15 minutes or so before she indignantly told me she was tired of being told what she needed to do. She just needed to take a nap. To stop worrying, let her get some rest, and she promised she'd call me later that night.

90 minutes later my brother called me. Mom was gone. He had frantically tried to resuscitate her for 20 minutes before an ambulance arrived at their home in the mountains. I would never get the phone call she had promised. A blood clot had broken loose and taken her. She was only 72.

I packed up my things, made the 12-hour drive, and did what needed to be done. I was the one she had left in charge of handling it all. I bottled up my emotions and got to work. I made certain the funeral was planned appropriately. Insurance companies were notified. I sorted through closets, talked to other family members, and filed documents. I pretended to be the strong one for family and friends. Then we buried her and said goodbye.

That was the moment I decided to give up on everything. I had become the quitter I said I never would be.

I was completely broken.

When I finally got home, I was exhausted in every possible way. I had made the decision to quit everything. Kayaking, physical therapy, my business- even my emotions. I told my husband I didn't have anything left in me. I wanted to sell my boat, close my business, and cancel my trip to Arizona. He insisted I wait and encouraged me to go on the event trip. I was too tired to argue, so I found myself on a plane 7 days after Mom's funeral, wondering what I was doing and how I was going to get through it. I figured there was nothing left to lose. I had already lost everything.

It's in that moment when you've finally reached your version of rock bottom, one of two things will happen.

You'll either allow yourself to self-destruct, or you'll allow yourself to become vulnerable.

If you decide to become vulnerable, that's when the magic starts to happen.

I didn't know that at the time. I always thought you had to be strong and never show your weaknesses. I had no idea vulnerability was a strength. The only thing I knew was I didn't have it in me to be anything else. There were no walls left to hide behind. I was wide open.

Call it divine intervention, The Universe calling, "the nudge", or even my mom deciding from the afterlife she had seen and heard enough. Whatever it was, things were about to change thanks to a series of conversations. What would normally be considered small-talk or just chit-chat.

Except these conversations created impact like a lightning bolt going through me. It's what I now refer to as *The Power of a 5-Minute Conversation*. They're simple chats with any-one, even total strangers, that can change a life. Something as simple as giving a much-needed smile or a boost of confi-dence to someone during the course of their day, all the way to giving someone an idea for a business…or even saving a life. The person saying it might not even remember what they said minutes later, but their words create dynamic effects in the lives of the person that is listening. That's what happened to me.

It started with a woman named Lea Woodford. I had paid attention to her career in both television and radio prior to the 365 Driven Advance event, so I was excited when Tony announced she would be a speaker.

I don't know what prompted me to call out to her on the first night and invite her to sit at the table I was at. It turned out she already knew my friend Cynthia who was sitting with me, which made breaking the ice far easier. Once the conver-sation started, it was as if I had known her my entire life. We talked about shared experiences in the radio and television in-dustries. We talked about favorite celebrities we had been for-tunate enough to meet and work with over the years. We talked about similarities growing up, and some of the issues we had to overcome. Then came the moment she asked me what I was doing now. I told her I had started a copywriting business almost a year ago but had decided to pause it to regroup after my injury and Mom's passing.

She looked at me as if I had spoken a foreign language before saying, "But you're a public speaker. Why aren't you professionally speaking TO other people instead of FOR them?" It literally felt like I got hit by lightning. That idea simply hadn't been one I'd entertained. I didn't know how to answer her.

She wouldn't be the only one that night to stun me with that observation.

Kevin Tetz was another speaker at the Advance. I had seen him on a couple of automotive shows on Spike TV. My Mom's husband Fred was a huge fan of his. He also had been the front man for the Glam Rock hair band Nova Rex back in the 80's. I knew he'd have fantastic stories to tell, so I wasted no time starting up a conversation with him while watching a few others shoot pool.

After several minutes of lively chat trading concert shenanigans and adventures over the years in our entertainment careers, he asked what I was doing now. Once again, there was a look of disbelief when I said I was writing copy. He told me my voice stood out in a crowded room and commanded attention. It was a voice that made people want to listen and be part of the conversation. Why, with all my experience, wasn't I using it?

Boom. Lightning strike #2. I told him I didn't think I was good enough, but it was something I would have to consider going forward.

I didn't sleep well that night. I kept replaying those conversations in my head trying to process what they had said.

That was the day before the Advance even got rolling officially.

That next morning, I headed to the conference room to listen to the keynote speakers. That's when I had my first experience with Princeton Clark. Princeton is a larger-than-life speaker and author who had worked with Tony Robbins before creating his own business. When this man speaks, you can't help but notice.

So, when he started talking about his spirituality and meditations to calm his mind for focus and clarity, I paid attention. I worked up enough courage to catch him on a break when he was alone in the entryway to ask him what he would suggest to help me quiet my mind and gain some perspective.

He looked at me for a moment with a warm smile, and said, "What you need to do is let your inner child come back out and have a voice." I teared up a bit and told him I didn't want to ever go back to my childhood. He just smiled and told me I'd never be happy and find success until I listened to her and made peace.

And there was lightning bolt #3. I had buried her decades ago, or so I thought. I had lost who I was because I didn't want to remember who SHE was...a little girl with a voice and big dreams. I walled her up because I didn't like the feeling of being hurt. The truth is, I was being hurt anyway. Likely more so than if I had just acknowledged her in the first place. I saw that childlike vulnerability as a weakness.

I was wrong. Your vulnerability can be your greatest strength. It makes you human and allows you to connect with others. And that connection let's others hear your voice. It lets you hear your own voice to help guide you to where you need to be. To guide you to your own happiness and success.

Later that day those same three people that had jolted me to the core cornered me at the same time and asked me, "Are you finally about done with all of your bullshit?" For the first time in years, I could smile and say yes, I was officially over all of it. I made a promise then that I would never go back to the way I had been when I had first arrived. I went from having a frog in my throat to BEING the **F.R.O.G.** IN the throat, refusing to give up.

And it all happened because of a few, powerful, 5-minute conversations.

Sometimes that's all it takes, a simple 5-minute conversation. My world changed in those few minutes. If I'm fortunate, I'll be able to be that change for someone else too. Or maybe you'll be the voice someone else needs to hear. Never be afraid to strike up a conversation and truly listen. There's magic in the simplest of words. Pay attention, and you'll see the powerful impact they can make.

IT'S NOT EASY BEING GREEN

"No one remembers who you were when you did all your things." I was told that by someone recently.

Not true.

I remember who I was.

I know who I am.

And that's really all that matters; all it takes to keep pushing that needle forward and finding my wings to soar again.

This is definitely a new experience. I'm not an expert at being a **F.R.O.G.** And that's the secret.

None of us are.

Kermit the Frog sings, "It's not easy being green." He's right. It's a journey full of hurdles and setbacks. You're going to slip and fall along the way. You might even fall into the trappings of being a **F.I.S.H.** or a **S.T.O.R.K.** from time to time.

The important thing is that you recognize it and then remember:

- Who you are
- What you love

- How you got there
- The steps that helped you along the way
- YOU ARE A **F.R.O.G.**

You only have to take that **L.E.A.P** to get past your hurdles.

Even Superman needs to take that **L.E.A.P.** before he can fly.

It's too easy to fall into the trap of thinking you're a victim of something: Of intimidation, discrimination, hostility, other people, and unfortunate situations.

The only thing I was ever a victim of was myself. I was a **F.I.S.H.** who was too often getting in her own way. That realization might be the biggest hurdle a person has to **L.E.A.P.** over. Sometimes in order to become a bona fide **F.R.O.G.**, we have to **F**inally **R**efuse our **OWN G**arbage.

I'm not mad at the people that "wronged" me anymore, nor at the situations that hurt and slowed me down. Okay, maybe a little mad. I'm human after all. What I'm mostly upset by is that I allowed outside influences to make me question myself. I'm mad at ME. But even that is something I'm getting past and learning to let go. I'm becoming grateful for all of it. Because without these people and experiences, I wouldn't have developed the skills and grown into the person I am currently. While I'm not certain I'd be ready to sit down over coffee and have a friendly conversation with some of the characters in my past, I don't wish them any ill-will either. Their situation wasn't mine. They likely were facing their own hurdles. For all I know, I was every bit as much a **S.T.O.R.K.** for them as they were for me.

I wouldn't want to repeat the situations I went through, nor would I wish them on others. But I'm not sorry I went through them. Even the hardest lessons give you a gift if you're willing to learn from them. The wealth of knowledge I've received has been priceless.

I never did grow up to be the next Wolfman Jack or Casey Kasem. I did something better. I grew and stepped into my own light. And while I won't be counting down your weekly favorites, or having people howl along with my antics, perhaps I can be that friendly voice coming out of nowhere to touch someone I haven't met yet. One person who needs to be reminded they know how to get over life's hurdles if they're just willing to **L.E.A.P.**

Maybe that one person is you.

I'm not here to tell you what you need to do or give you a step-by-step plan to make all your dreams come true. If I did that, I'd be doing you a disservice and it likely wouldn't work for you. Instead, I'll leave you with one last thought and observation.

The biggest mistake I had in the past was thinking I needed someone else to turn me into a success. Somehow my ability to achieve great things was dependent on someone else making it happen for me. And the measure of success and greatness was determined by someone else's benchmarks.

What I've come to KNOW is that it never was anywhere except within myself. My success, my achievements, have all been dependent on my willingness to act, to have faith in myself, and to decide what was truly important in my life.

When you can listen to your inner voice, that invisible voice, it will tell you exactly what will make you happy and successful. And when you listen to it, you will automatically take the steps needed to get there. You will be faced with set-backs, **S.T.O.R.K.S**, and hurdles. But a hurdle is just an object you can **L.E.A.P.** over. And a **S.T.O.R.K.** is nothing but a big, stupid bird that can't swallow you unless you let it.

That's not to say you should shut everyone out. You aren't meant to be alone. Just because **F.I.S.H.** swim in schools doesn't mean you need to step away and figure everything out on your own. **F.R.O.G.**s hang out together. In fact, **F.R.O.G.**s hang out in groups called ARMIES. I think it's fitting in this case. I needed those other **F.R.O.G.**s to wake me up and help me remember what I already had inside of me.

Surround yourself with other **F.R.O.G.**s who have your back while you soldier on and complete your mission in life. Surround yourself with an army of supportive individuals who stand WITH you on your path. Not in your way like a hurdle.

Being a **F.R.O.G.** means adapting and growing over your lifetime. You transform yourself along the way.

So, what is the summary of what I've learned so far on the way to my own successful finish?

1. Believe in the *Power of a 5-Minute Conversation.*
2. **C.R.O.A.K.** when necessary.
3. Life can hit you harder than Sally Halbmaier with a spelling book. Don't be afraid to take the swing and get back up.
4. When that hurdle arrives, flex your jumping legs and **L.E.A.P.**

5. Focus on being your own **F.R.O.G.**, not on what someone else thinks you should be.
6. When things start going wrong, take a moment and make certain you aren't turning into your own **S.T.O.R.K.**
7. If you find you ARE your own **S.T.O.R.K.**, give yourself some grace and understand no one is perfect, and you can change your situation.
8. The secret to your success and happiness isn't in the hands of someone else. It's inside of you. You just have to listen to your inner voice. REALLY listen to it.
9. Your vulnerability is your superpower. Don't be afraid of it.
10. Above all else, NEVER GIVE UP. And always "order the pie."

Be the **F.R.O.G.** in life's throat.

AM I STILL FEELING FROGGY?

I can finally say with great certainty I'm living a **F.R.O.G.** life. I still have to catch myself from time-to-time, so I don't slip backwards into the **F.I.S.H.** tank. Being a **F.R.O.G.** takes work, but it's worth it. For the first time in my life, I can say I'm truly happy and confident. It's a joy living each day.

How have things changed?

In less than a year I've written this book that has healed me in ways I didn't know were even possible. I've finally confronted the baggage I've accrued over my lifetime and worked through it instead of burying it deep down. Thank you for being part of that process.

I've relaunched my business. I'm a Communication Strategist hired to connect your voice and your message with your ideal client or audience. Both the group coaching and individual customized strategies are incredibly fulfilling. It's a huge joy watching the eyes of the people I have the privilege of connecting with light up when they finally discover how to get their voice heard properly and connect on levels they didn't believe were possible.

I've spoken to audiences globally about *The Power of A 5-Minute Conversation* and am speaking on stages about how to better connect with your target audience, both personally and professionally.

I've been featured in *Speaker Life* magazine giving tips on how to become a better podcast host and guest.

I'm back behind the microphone and have a podcast of my own. Every day playing behind the microphone and connecting to others brings me pure joy.

I've also created a professional voice-over business providing scriptwriting, audio, and editing for marketing videos, social media and YouTube, radio and television commercial production, and audio books. The collaborations and creative process has been so much fun.

My relationship with my kids has strengthened. I've got my oldest daughter, her husband, and my "grandpuppy" (French Bulldog named Po) close to home again and we have reconnected in ways I didn't think I'd ever have. Devon is once again my happiness. I'm hoping it won't be much longer before I can be a "Glamma" to more than just the dog.

Katy, the youngest, has begun interning with me to learn the voice over business. She's not as thrilled about editing as I am, but she's good at it. She understands that if you're going to provide a voice, you have to know how to use the equipment to record and send it. She's so smart. She completed her first semester at college with all A's and B's and will head back in the fall. She's a beautiful young lady. She is my strength and my motivation. She fills my soul.

Chris and I are hitting 30 years of marriage together (yes, combined from marriages #1 and #2). It's not easy every day, but it's certainly worth it. He is still working with the Air Force. I maintain he's working with aliens. He continues to tell me that information is "classified."

We are looking forward to some great life adventures including Indy, Formula One, and even NASCAR races (I love Kimi Raikkonen), more trips to the mountains to narrow down where we will have our retirement home, and kayak races.

Yes, I'm back in the kayak. I love being on the water. I'm finally accomplishing the races I missed with the injuries…and I'm back stronger than ever!

Above all else, I'm back to being "me." Acknowledging and listening to my "inner little Sheral" voice. "We" work as a team finding the opportunities and experiences to create joy and balance in our life and providing value and motivation to others.

CONTACT ME

If you've enjoyed this book, I would love to hear your experiences of becoming your own **F.R.O.G.** Send me an email at sher@speakingwithsher.com. Please also share an honest review on Amazon or your favorite online retailer.

If you'd like to explore other ways to connect with me professionally, please visit my website:
www.speakingwithsher.com

GLOSSARY OF TERMS

S.T.O.R.K. Situational Taker Of Rational Knowledge

F.I.S.H. Folks In Search of Help

F.R.O.G. Folks Refusing Other's Garbage

C.R.O.A.K. Challenge Really Obnoxious A-holes and Kill-Joys

L.E.A.P. Look/Learn, Educate/Evolve, Act, Practice/Participate

H.O.P.P.E.R. Hoping Our Problems Promptly Exit Routinely

The Power of a 5 Minute Conversation Words that are said so casually by others that they might not even remember saying them. Words that have the power to change your life.